To Bowie, you motivate me every day to get out of bed at 5 am (not by choice!) and you inspired the focus of this book, with its simple and easy recipes. You also made a wonderful taste tester for lots of these recipes and are my toughest critic.

Simple
(mostly) VEGAN
KITCHEN

Ellie Bullen

plum Pan Macmillan Australia

Contents

INTRODUCTION

Hello! My name is Ellie, or as some of you may know me, Elsa, from my online platform, Elsa's Wholesome Life. I am passionate about creating and sharing wholesome plant-based recipes and am so happy to be back with my third cookbook, which is filled with simple, quick and delicious meals for you and your family.

In case you are new here, let me tell you a little about myself. I grew up in the small beachside town of Lennox Head, in northern New South Wales, Australia. Growing up in this beautiful environment gave me an appreciation for nature and a healthy, active lifestyle. From an early age I was interested in cooking, food and health, and I eventually went on to study Nutrition and Dietetics at university. While studying for my degree, I began creating recipes and sharing them online, and this is how Elsa's Wholesome Life was born.

I am a self-taught cook and over the years I have continued to build on my skills, learning about food through travelling, taking cooking lessons overseas and my own experimentation. I enjoy helping people to become more confident in the kitchen, not only through my website and cookbooks, but also through my YouTube channel.

One of the best things you can do for your health is to eat fewer processed foods, so it brings me joy to help people learn to cook wholesome meals using simple, fresh ingredients and notice the positive impact on their health. I am also proud to bring the knowledge I have from being a dietitian and nutritionist to the recipes I create, ensuring that every one of them is delicious, balanced and nutritionally sound.

My first cookbook, *Elsa's Wholesome Life*, was published soon after I graduated from university, followed by *The Global Vegan*, which was filled with recipes inspired by the years I spent living and travelling overseas. Since those days of travelling the world, life has taken a beautiful turn. My husband Alex and I moved back to Australia, settled on the Gold Coast and bought our first home together.

Not long after moving into our new home, the pandemic hit. I was a few months pregnant and like many people, spent a lot more time at home, in and out of lockdowns. During this time, I found joy in simple daily routines and fell in love all over again with the pleasures of home cooking. I also felt even more connected to my online community through doing weekly live cooking demonstrations, which I loved so much.

Alex and I then welcomed our son Bowie into the world in July 2020 and our lives became a lot more chaotic, with much less sleep and a lot less time to cook meals! This book was born out of my desire to cook delicious meals fast, and is very much a reflection of my current life stage as a busy working mum. I wanted to simplify my recipes so that they contained fewer ingredients and steps and required shorter cooking times, while not sacrificing on flavour or nutrition. So here they are: simple, wholesome and delicious family meals that you will be able to whip up quickly and easily, even on a busy weeknight.

I have included some baby and toddler friendly recipes for those who are on a similar journey to me and are looking for new meal ideas for their little ones. There are hearty brekkies, simple snacks to make in your air fryer and loads of main meals, including ideas for your slow cooker so that you can work all day but still come home to a satisfying cooked meal. And of course, I couldn't live without a treat now and then, so you'll find some yummy sweets and drinks in here, too. Apart from the occasional inclusion of honey, which I have started using sparingly in my cooking, all of these recipes are entirely plant based and bursting with nutrition.

I hope you enjoy using the recipes in this book as much as I enjoyed creating them. I am excited to hear what you think and hope that some of these meals become family favourites in your household, just like they are in mine.

x Ellie

My (Almost) Vegan Pantry

Here are some of the ingredients that I always keep in my pantry, fridge and freezer.
Stock your kitchen with these and a delicious meal will never be far away.
All of the ingredients below are vegan, except for honey, which I have started using
sparingly in some dishes. You can always substitute it with maple syrup to
keep things completely vegan.

Açai

Açai berries are native to South America and they
are high in antioxidants and fibre. Açai is available
from health food stores and some supermarkets
and is normally sold in sachets of frozen puree.
I love making açai bowls (see page 22) for brekkie
through the summer months, as they are a
wonderful fresh start to the day.

Aquafaba

Aquafaba is the liquid in canned chickpeas that is
often poured right out of the can and down the
drain. When I first learned about the idea of using
aquafaba in recipes, I thought it was a really
strange concept as I found chickpea water a little
bit stinky. However, aquafaba is actually a good
egg white substitute and I love finding a way to use
an otherwise discarded ingredient! You may see it
replace eggs in vegan cocktails, meringues and
aioli or mayo.

Berries

I always have a stash of berries in my fridge and/or
freezer, for using in smoothies, baking or to scatter
over pancakes or waffles. Berries are high in
antioxidants and are a fabulous healthy treat for
babies and toddlers, too.

Buckinis

Buckinis are buckwheat kernels that have been
soaked and then dried to activate them. They
can be sprinkled on smoothies, added to muesli,
or used in all kinds of sweet treats, such as my
choc-drizzle muesli cups (see page 242). They are
available from some supermarkets and health
food stores.

Canned lentils, chickpeas & beans

Canned legumes are an excellent staple to have in your pantry to create healthy vegan meals for the whole family. They are cost effective and a wonderful source of plant protein and fibre. Of course, if you've got the time, you can cook dried ones from scratch, but when you are short on time, it's so convenient to be able to grab a can from the pantry. I use legumes in all kinds of meals, for breakfast, lunch and dinner, whether it's baked beans (see page 79), crispy chickpeas (see page 137) or a Mexican-inspired black bean bake (see page 174).

Chia seeds

These seeds are packed with nutrition. They contain all nine essential amino acids, and have a fantastic fat profile, as they are high in omega-3 fatty acids. They're also high in fibre and make a great egg replacement as they soak up the liquid and become gelatinous. Try them in my choc–chia pudding (see page 25) for a delicious brekkie.

Chipotle seasoning

Chipotle is actually a jalapeño chilli that has been smoke-dried, hence the smoky flavour. The chillies are dried and ground to create a smoky seasoning that adds loads of flavour to a range of dishes, especially my corn ribs (see page 92). You'll find chipotle seasoning in the Mexican or spice section of supermarkets and fine food stores.

Flax seeds

Flax seeds are another seed I like to include in my daily diet. It's important to use flaxseed meal or grind down your flax seeds yourself to ensure you get maximum nutrition from them. I use ground flax meal in some recipes as an egg replacement. In a similar way to chia seeds, it absorbs water and takes on a gelatinous egg-like texture. Flax seeds

are high in omega-3 fatty acids. Store them in the fridge in an airtight container for maximum freshness.

Hemp seeds

Hemp seeds are the seed of the cannabis/hemp plant. They do not contain THC (the principal psychoactive constituent of cannabis) and they are legal here in Australia. I once visited a hemp farm just prior to harvest and learned all about this super food. Hemp seeds are rich in protein and omega-3 fatty acids. I try to eat 1 tablespoon daily, sprinkled over almost any sweet or savoury dish!

Jalapeños

I adore Mexican food so I always keep some pickled jalapeños in my cupboard for adding to burritos (see page 55), quesadillas (see page 121) or even toasties (see page 66). Pickled jalapeños are available from the Mexican section at the supermarket or you can purchase them fresh and pickle them yourself following the pickled onion recipe on page 227.

Matcha powder

Matcha powder is made from green tea leaves that have been ground into a fine powder. It is very high in antioxidants and I love adding it to smoothies (see page 30).

Mushrooms

Mushrooms are a fabulous addition to any diet, but particularly for vegetarians and vegans, as they add real depth of flavour, an interesting texture and great nutritional value. I use many different types of mushrooms in my cooking, including brown, button and shiitake. If you're looking for new ideas with mushrooms, try my mushroom and leek risotto (see page 160) or mushroom, chive and three cheese toastie (see page 62).

Nutritional yeast

Nutritional yeast is made from deactivated yeast flakes that have been fortified with vitamin B12. It is different to baker's or brewer's yeast as it does not rise or bubble. Nutritional yeast has a savoury, cheesy flavour so is often added to vegan cheeses or sauces. It can also be sprinkled over salads and added to patties and pasta sauces. Try my vegan parmesan on page 216.

Nuts & seeds

Keep your favourite nuts and seeds well stocked in the pantry in order to add texture, flavour and nutrition to any meal. Ground almonds are great for baking, while any nuts or seeds can be added to smoothies for a boost of protein and healthy fats. Sprinkle salads with toasted nuts and seeds for a delicious crunchy texture.

Plant milk, yoghurt & cream

I use a wide variety of plant milks, including soy, oat and coconut milk, which are all readily available from supermarkets and health food stores. For yoghurt, I prefer coconut yoghurts, in particular Coyo brand, while oat cream is my go-to for adding a smooth, rich element to sauces (see page 167) or to serve with desserts. You can find Oatly brand oat cream in some supermarkets and health food stores.

Quinoa

Quinoa is my favourite high-protein whole grain. It is actually a seed but has a nutritional profile closer to a grain, and originates from South America. It contains all nine essential amino acids, is gluten free and high in fibre. It comes in black, white and red varieties, but I often buy the tri-colour quinoa. It is quick to cook, so it's great to have on hand for family dinners, such as my sweet and spicy cauliflower salad (see page 154).

Shichimi togarashi

Shichimi togarashi is a popular Japanese spice mix that commonly contains seven different spices, often including chilli, sesame seeds and ginger. It is available from Asian grocers and adds a yummy flavour to Asian dishes, such as my simple creamy ramen on page 170.

Sriracha chilli sauce

This spicy chilli sauce is a great one to keep in the pantry as it's so easy to add to the top of noodle dishes, stir-fries, eggs or any savoury dish that you want to add a kick to. Sriracha is readily available from supermarkets and Asian grocers.

Sweeteners

COCONUT SUGAR
Coconut sugar is a sweetener that comes from the sap of the coconut palm tree, not the actual coconut. It is very popular in cooking, and is my go-to sugar in baked goods, such as chocolate and walnut brownies (see page 252), which are so decadent and delicious!

HONEY
I recently started incorporating honey into my diet and, while strict vegans choose not to eat it, I really enjoy supporting local bee keepers and purchasing it from my local farmers' market for use in a variety of dishes. It is great in sauces, on top of smoothie bowls, and I particularly love it in my lemon pepper cauliflower (see page 130). If you don't eat honey, there are plenty of vegan sweeteners, such as maple syrup, which will work just as well.

MAPLE SYRUP
Pure maple syrup is a liquid sweetener with a delicious caramel flavour. It is very popular in sauces and baking. I use it in my ginger–caramel pudding (see page 264) and on top of pancakes (see page 44) and waffles (see page 51).

MEDJOOL DATES

I use medjool dates a lot in baking and smoothies. In comparison to other dates, medjool dates are a fresh fruit that are gooey, contain a pit and have a rich caramel flavour. They are the base of one of my favourite desserts, date 'snickers' (see page 257), but I also use them in a variety of sweet dishes.

Tempeh

Tempeh is an excellent plant-based protein source. It is a traditional food of Indonesia and is made from the fermentation of soy beans. It is a less processed, healthier version of tofu and is rich in both protein and fibre as well as many vitamins and minerals. If you've never eaten tempeh, try my baked tempeh sticks (see page 98) – they are so quick to whip up and make the perfect crispy afternoon snack.

Teriyaki sauce

Teriyaki is a sweet and salty Japanese sauce that is brilliant for bringing flavour to Asian-inspired dishes, such as my crispy teriyaki tofu bowl (see page 150). It's readily available from supermarkets.

Textured vegetable protein (TVP)

Textured vegetable protein or TVP (also known as textured soy protein) is made from de-fatted soy in the process of making soy bean oil. It is high in protein and often used as a meat replacement as, when cooked, it resembles the texture of minced beef. It is commonly used in veggie spaghetti, pies, tacos or hamburger patties. Since it is more processed than tofu and tempeh I tend to use TVP only occasionally, but its resemblance to minced meat makes it very great in dishes such as veggie con carne (see page 190).

Vegan butter & cheese

I use vegan butter for baking and cooking, and vegan cheeses, such as parmesan, feta and cheddar, to add to toasties, waffles, burritos and bakes. While it's not hard to make your own vegan cheese (see page 216 for some recipes) they are also readily available from supermarkets and health food stores, so feel free to save yourself time by choosing store-bought versions.

My (Almost) Vegan Pantry

Handy Equipment

Having the right tools can save you time and energy in the kitchen. Here is my list of essential items that I couldn't live without.

Air fryer

I had heard a lot about air fryers, so I recently decided to invest in one myself and I absolutely love it! It makes cooking so much easier and most things fry in half the time they would take in the oven. I've included a handful of air fryer recipes in this book (see pages 124–38) and I highly recommend purchasing one if you are struggling to find the time to cook delicious, healthy food!

Blender

I love my high-speed blender and use it many times a day to make smoothies, pikelets, soups, sauces, sweets or even my own plant milks.

Mandoline & julienne peeler

Mandolines and julienne peelers are useful for thinly slicing or julienning vegetables and fruits really quickly. They are easy to use, save lots of time and are inexpensive.

Non-stick frying pan

A good-quality non-stick frying pan is essential in any kitchen – I recommend buying the best quality you can afford as it will last longer and make flipping pancakes or frying veggie patties much easier and more enjoyable!

Slow cooker

Slow cooking has been a game-changer for me with my busy lifestyle, running my own business plus being a mum. It can often be overwhelming to prepare a hearty meal after a big day of work. I love my slow cooker because I can put a delicious, healthy meal on to cook in the morning and come home to it after a long day. I have included a bunch of my favourite slow cooker recipes in this book (see pages 178–95).

Açai bowl with all the toppings

Choc—chia pudding

Everyday banana pikelets

On-the-run brekkie smoothies

Simple blueberry bircher

Choc-chip banana muffins

Apple crumble breakfast bake

Banana & cinnamon porridge

Pancakes, your way

Blueberry & coconut brekkie crumble

Ridiculously good waffles

Best-ever brekkie burrito

Tofu scramble with spinach & cherry tomatoes

Mushroom, chive & three cheese toastie

Avocado, kale & pesto toastie

Spicy pepperoni toastie

Baked bean & cheese toastie

Hash browns

Baked tofu & avo shakshuka

Spicy tomato chickpeas on toast with feta

Cheesy baked beans with roasted capsicum

Brekkie

Açai bowl
with all the toppings

Açai bowls are a summer breakfast staple in our home – they are such a simple, fresh start to the day. I love mixing things up: use the toppings below as a guide and feel free to swap in different ingredients.

Serves 2 / gfo (use gf granola)

2 × 100 g sachets of frozen pure açai
200 g chopped frozen banana
3 tablespoons liquid, such as coconut water, coconut milk or fruit juice

Toppings for each bowl
3 tablespoons granola
1 teaspoon desiccated coconut
5 banana slices
handful of berries of your choice
1 tablespoon peanut butter
1 teaspoon honey (or rice malt syrup for a vegan option)

Smash the açai sachets on your work surface to break them up (this helps with the blending process). Empty the sachets into a blender and add the frozen banana and your chosen liquid. Blend until thick and smooth.

Divide the açai mixture between two bowls and top with the granola, desiccated coconut, fruit, peanut butter and a drizzle of sweetener.

Tip

For the perfect açai bowls, always use frozen banana and don't add too much liquid. I never add ice as it melts and turns the açai mixture watery.

Choc-chia
pudding

Chia pudding is such a simple and delicious breakfast, but adding cacao takes it to a whole other level. I love this breakfast as it's so easy to make, and also doubles as a quick dessert.

Serves 1 / gfo (use gf plant milk)

3 tablespoons chia seeds
250 ml (1 cup) plant-based milk (such as oat or soy)
2 teaspoons maple syrup
1 tablespoon cacao powder (use 1 teaspoon for toddlers)
1 heaped tablespoon natural coconut yoghurt
1 tablespoon coconut flakes
handful of raspberries
1 teaspoon vegan chocolate chips or cacao nibs

Combine the chia seeds, plant-based milk and maple syrup in a bowl, then set aside in the fridge for 10 minutes to set.

Remove the bowl from the fridge, add the cacao powder and mix well. Spoon the chia pudding into a glass and top with the coconut yoghurt, coconut flakes, raspberries and chocolate chips or cacao nibs. Enjoy straight away.

Everyday
banana pikelets

Both baby and adult friendly, these pikelets are such a hit with my son.
They are also an easy on-the-go breakfast or snack to prepare ahead
and enjoy over the following days. Simple to make and absolutely delicious,
they are sure to please the whole family. Serve with your choice of toppings.

Makes 15–20 small pikelets

½ banana
310 ml (1¼ cups) soy milk
1 tablespoon flaxseed meal
½ teaspoon vanilla extract
150 g (1 cup) plain flour
1½ teaspoons baking powder
pinch of sea salt
2 teaspoons apple cider vinegar
olive oil or vegan butter, for cooking

To serve
seasonal fruit
peanut butter
natural coconut yoghurt
hemp seeds
maple syrup (optional; omit for babies)

Place the banana, soy milk, flaxseed meal and vanilla extract in a blender and blend until smooth. Pour into a large mixing bowl.

Sift the flour, baking powder and salt into the wet mixture and gently fold the ingredients together, ensuring not to overmix. Once the batter is half mixed, add the apple cider vinegar and mix until smooth.

Heat a frying pan over medium–high heat and grease with a drizzle of olive oil or vegan butter. Add heaped tablespoons of the batter to the pan and cook the pikelets for about 45 seconds each side, until cooked through and golden.

Transfer the pikelets to plates and serve with your choice of seasonal fruit, peanut butter, coconut yoghurt, hemp seeds and maple syrup, if desired.

Store the pikelets in an airtight container in the fridge for up to 3 days.

Baby/toddler friendly (omit the chocolate chips)

On-the-run
brekkie smoothies

Smoothies are such a staple in my diet as they are an easy, fast and filling breakfast option. Here, I've shared recipes for four of my favourites, each one delicious in its own way!

Raspberry ripe

Serves 1 / gf

1 large frozen banana (150 g)
125 g (1 cup) frozen raspberries
2 tablespoons cacao powder
2 medjool dates, pitted
3 tablespoons desiccated coconut
250 ml (1 cup) coconut milk
½ cup crushed ice
Toppings (optional)
raspberries
vegan chocolate chips
desiccated coconut

Place all of the ingredients and 3 tablespoons of water in a blender and blend for 30 seconds. Pour into a glass and serve with your choice of toppings.

Matcha green

Serves 1 / gfo (use gf plant milk instead of oat milk)

1 large frozen banana (150 g)
½ zucchini (70 g), chopped
250 ml (1 cup) oat milk
1–2 medjool dates, pitted
1 tablespoon hemp seeds, plus extra to serve
2 teaspoons matcha powder
45 g (1 cup firmly packed) baby spinach leaves
½ cup crushed ice

Place all of the ingredients in a blender and blend for 30 seconds. Pour into a glass, top with some extra hemp seeds and serve.

Toddler friendly (omit the chocolate chips)

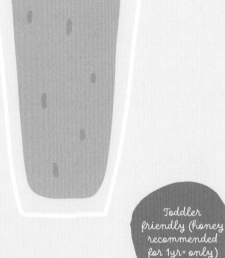

Toddler friendly (honey recommended for 1yr+ only)

Peanut butter cup

Serves 1 / gf

1 frozen banana (130 g)
2 medjool dates, pitted
2 tablespoons peanut butter, plus extra
  to serve
2 teaspoons cacao powder
1 cup crushed ice
250 ml (1 cup) soy milk
2 teaspoons vegan chocolate chips or
  cacao nibs, to serve

Place all of the ingredients except the chocolate chips or cacao nibs in a blender and blend for 30 seconds. Pour into a glass, top with some extra peanut butter and the chocolate chips or cacao nibs and serve.

Simple banana

Serves 1 / gfo (omit the oats)

1 large frozen banana (150 g)
1 cup crushed ice
½ teaspoon ground cinnamon, plus extra
  to serve
2 teaspoons honey (or maple syrup for
  a vegan option)
375 ml (1½ cups) soy milk
35 g (⅓ cup) rolled oats (optional)
1 tablespoon hemp seeds (optional)

Place all of the ingredients in a blender and blend for 30 seconds. Pour into a glass, top with some extra cinnamon and enjoy!

Raspberry ripe smoothie, see page 30

Matcha green smoothie, see page 30

Peanut butter cup smoothie, see page 31

Simple banana smoothie, see page 31

Simple
blueberry bircher

This delicious bircher muesli includes healthy omega fatty acids, and you can add any or all of the topping suggestions. If you omit the honey or maple syrup, this recipe is great for little babes starting solids as it has a beautiful soft texture. Bowie loves eating this for breakfast and we also stir his probiotic powder into the bowl every morning.

Serves 4

155 g (1 cup) blueberries (fresh or frozen)
⅓ teaspoon ground cinnamon
200 g (2 cups) quick oats
4 tablespoons hemp, flax or chia seeds
  (or a mixture of all three)
625 ml (2½ cups) soy milk
125 g (½ cup) vanilla coconut yoghurt
2 scoops of baby probiotics (optional)
Topping suggestions
nut butter
crushed nuts
hemp seeds
toasted coconut flakes
seasonal fruit
natural coconut yoghurt
granola
honey (or maple syrup for a vegan option)

Place the blueberries in a large bowl and roughly mash with a fork. Add the remaining ingredients except the baby probiotics (if using) and stir together until well combined. Cover and refrigerate overnight.

The next morning, spoon the bircher into bowls and add the baby probiotics to your baby's serve, if desired. Enjoy as is or serve with some or all of the topping suggestions.

choc-chip banana
muffins

These banana muffins are a huge hit with my family! Filled with delicious chocolate chips,
they are a fantastic and easy snack to prepare and enjoy throughout the week.

Makes 12

3 large bananas (about 325 g)
1 teaspoon vanilla extract
1 tablespoon flaxseed meal
80 ml (⅓ cup) maple syrup
80 ml (⅓ cup) olive oil
250 ml (1 cup) soy milk
300 g (2 cups) plain flour
2 teaspoons baking powder
pinch of sea salt
1 teaspoon ground cinnamon
3 tablespoons vegan chocolate chips

Preheat the oven to 170°C fan-forced. Grease a
12-hole cupcake tin (silicone moulds work best for
easy removal).

Place the banana, vanilla extract, flaxseed meal,
maple syrup and olive oil in a large bowl and mash
the banana with a fork. Add the soy milk and stir
well to combine, then set aside for 5 minutes to
allow the flaxseed meal to absorb the liquid.

Sift the flour, baking powder, salt and cinnamon into
the bowl and fold through the wet mixture until just
combined. Stir the chocolate chips into the batter.

Spoon the batter into the prepared cupcake
tin, until each hole or mould is three-quarters full,
then place the tin on a baking tray, transfer to
the oven and bake for about 15 minutes, until
a skewer inserted into one of the muffins comes
out clean. Allow the muffins to cool in the tin for
20 minutes before turning out onto a wire rack to
cool completely.

Store the muffins in an airtight container in the
pantry for up to 3 days.

Apple crumble
breakfast bake

Is there anything better than dessert for breakfast? This apple crumble is a quick, easy and hearty sweet dish that can be enjoyed at the start or the end of the day (or anywhere in between, to be honest). I often share this with my family and friends – everyone loves the flavour combination of apple and cinnamon.

Serves 4

2 granny smith apples, cored and finely diced
2 medjool dates, pitted and finely chopped
½ teaspoon ground cinnamon
1 teaspoon vanilla extract
100 g (1 cup) rolled oats
50 g (½ cup) almond meal
45 g (½ cup) desiccated coconut
⅓ teaspoon sea salt
2 tablespoons coconut sugar
2 tablespoons vegan butter
natural coconut yoghurt, to serve

Preheat the oven to 170°C fan-forced.

Place the apple, date, cinnamon and vanilla extract in a large bowl and mix well to combine. Transfer to a small baking dish.

Place the oats, almond meal, desiccated coconut, salt, coconut sugar and vegan butter in the bowl and mix with your hands until well combined. Scatter the oat mixture on top of the apple, then transfer to the oven and bake for about 25 minutes, until the crumble is golden brown.

Allow the crumble to cool until warm, then spoon onto plates and serve with a dollop of natural coconut yoghurt on the side.

Tip

This crumble also doubles as a dessert, so keep any leftovers in an airtight container in the fridge for when you are in need of something sweet after dinner. It will keep for up to 2 days.

Banana & cinnamon
porridge

We all adore porridge in our house. We enjoy it all year round, but especially in winter when the mornings are cool and we crave something warm to start the day. Lately, we've been loving topping our classic porridge with peanut butter, honey and seasonal fresh fruit. It's wholesome and filling enough to see everyone through to lunch.

Serves 2

1 banana
¼ teaspoon ground cinnamon
100 g (1 cup) rolled oats
500 ml (2 cups) soy milk, plus extra
  to serve
2 teaspoons flaxseed meal

To serve
peanut butter
honey (or maple syrup for a vegan option)
seasonal fruit

Mash the banana and cinnamon together in a small bowl and set aside.

Place a saucepan over medium–high heat. Add the oats, soy milk and flaxseed meal and cook, stirring constantly, for 8 minutes or until you have a creamy porridge. Add the mashed banana mixture and stir through for 30 seconds, then remove the pan from the heat.

Divide the porridge between two bowls and serve hot with extra milk, peanut butter, honey or maple syrup and seasonal fruit.

Pancakes,
your way

When choosing between chocolate chips or blueberries for your pancakes,
my question is always: why not have both? This recipe is so versatile –
simply make the batter and serve with your favourite toppings.

Serves 2 (makes 8 thick pancakes)

1 tablespoon apple cider vinegar
250 ml (1 cup) soy milk
150 g (1 cup) plain flour
2 teaspoons baking powder
½ teaspoon sea salt
1 tablespoon maple syrup, plus extra
  to serve (optional)
155 g (1 cup) blueberries and/or 3 tablespoons
  vegan chocolate chips
1 tablespoon vegan butter or olive oil,
  plus extra vegan butter to serve
seasonal fruit, to serve (optional)

Combine the apple cider vinegar and soy milk in a small bowl, then set aside for 2 minutes.

Sift the flour, baking powder and salt into a large bowl. Add the soy milk mixture and maple syrup and mix gently with a whisk until well combined. Add the blueberries and/or chocolate chips and combine.

Heat the vegan butter or olive oil in a frying pan over medium–high heat. Working in batches, add ⅓ cup of batter for each pancake to the pan and cook for 1 minute each side or until cooked through and golden brown.

Serve warm with some maple syrup and/or vegan butter and your choice of seasonal fruit, if desired.

Blueberry & coconut
brekkie crumble

My family and I cannot get enough of this wholesome blueberry crumble.
Not only does it taste incredible, it's also super simple to make and packed full of
nourishing ingredients, making it the perfect breakfast to share with loved ones.

Serves 4

155 g (1 cup) raw almonds
5 medjool dates, pitted
1 teaspoon vanilla extract
30 g (½ cup) coconut flakes, plus extra
  to serve
100 g (1 cup) rolled oats
¼ teaspoon sea salt
90 g (⅓ cup) almond butter
1½ tablespoons olive oil
310 g (2 cups) frozen blueberries, plus
  fresh blueberries to serve
vanilla coconut yoghurt, to serve

Preheat the oven to 160°C fan-forced.

Place the almonds, dates, vanilla extract, coconut flakes, oats and salt in a food processor and process until the mixture is mostly ground but still has a bit of texture. Remove 1 cup of the mixture from the food processor and set aside.

Add the almond butter and olive oil to the food processor and process for a further 30–60 seconds until well combined.

Pour the mixture into a small baking dish and press down lightly. Top with the frozen blueberries and reserved crumble mixture. Transfer to the oven and bake for 15 minutes or until golden.

Scatter some extra coconut flakes and a few fresh blueberries over the crumble and serve warm with vanilla coconut yoghurt.

Ridiculously good
waffles

Not only are waffles delicious, they are also super versatile! This recipe is a base that you can make sweet or savoury by adding different ingredients. I love serving savoury waffles with fresh herbs and vegan cream cheese, and sweet waffles with loads of vegan butter and maple syrup.

Savoury waffles

Serves 4

250 ml (1 cup) soy milk
1 tablespoon apple cider vinegar
150 g (1 cup) plain flour
2 teaspoons baking powder
1 tablespoon olive oil
½ teaspoon sea salt
1 tablespoon finely chopped chives
1 tablespoon finely chopped dill fronds
1 long red chilli, finely chopped
3 tablespoons finely chopped mushrooms
  of your choice
vegan butter or olive oil, for greasing

To serve
1 tablespoon vegan cream cheese
¼ avocado, cubed
chopped herbs of your choice
sliced long red chilli
Pickled Red Onion (see page 227)
1 tablespoon maple syrup
1 tablespoon balsamic vinegar
lime wedges (optional)

To make the savoury waffle batter, combine the soy milk and apple cider vinegar in a large bowl and leave for 2 minutes. Sift in the flour and baking powder, then mix well. Add the olive oil, salt, chives, dill, chilli and mushroom to the batter and stir well to combine.

Heat a waffle iron and lightly grease with vegan butter or olive oil.

Scoop enough of the batter into the waffle iron to cover the base and close the lid. Cook on high for 4½ minutes, then transfer the waffle to a plate and repeat with the remaining batter.

To serve, top the savoury waffles with the cream cheese, avocado, chopped herbs, chilli and pickled onion. Mix the maple syrup and balsamic vinegar in a small jug and pour over the top. Serve with lime wedges, if desired.

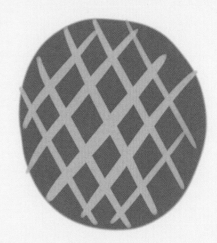

Sweet waffles

Serves 4

250 ml (1 cup) soy milk
1 tablespoon apple cider vinegar
150 g (1 cup) plain flour
2 teaspoons baking powder
1 tablespoon maple syrup
¼ teaspoon sea salt
vegan butter or olive oil, for greasing
To serve
vegan butter
fresh berries of your choice
maple syrup

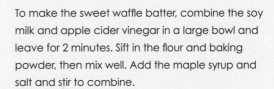

To make the sweet waffle batter, combine the soy milk and apple cider vinegar in a large bowl and leave for 2 minutes. Sift in the flour and baking powder, then mix well. Add the maple syrup and salt and stir to combine.

Heat a waffle iron and lightly grease with vegan butter or olive oil.

Scoop enough of the batter into the waffle iron to cover the base and close the lid. Cook on high for 4½ minutes, then transfer the waffle to a plate and repeat with the remaining batter.

To serve, top the sweet waffles with vegan butter and your choice of fresh berries. Pour over a little extra maple syrup and enjoy!

Savoury waffles,
see page 50

Sweet waffles,
see page 51

Best-ever
brekkie burrito

Nothing quite hits the spot like a breakfast burrito. Although you can add any number of ingredients to your tortillas, the combination here of hearty potato, punchy tomato and jalapeño salsa and creamy tofu scramble makes for a nourishing breakfast that is one of my absolute favourites in this book.

Serves 2 / gfo (use gf tortillas)

300 g potato, cut into 1 cm cubes
1 tablespoon olive oil
½ teaspoon sea salt
½ teaspoon smoked paprika
1 tablespoon finely chopped coriander root
2 large flour tortillas
1 avocado, mashed
2 tablespoons grated vegan cheese

Tofu scramble
300 g silken tofu
1 teaspoon olive oil
1 teaspoon vegetable stock powder
1 tablespoon nutritional yeast
¼ teaspoon ground turmeric

Tomato & jalapeño salsa
2 tomatoes, deseeded and finely diced
1 fresh jalapeño, deseeded and finely diced
2 tablespoons finely chopped coriander leaves and stalks
finely grated zest and juice of ½ lime
¼ teaspoon sea salt

To serve
coriander leaves
sliced fresh jalapeño
Pickled Red Onion (see page 227)
lime wedges

In a small bowl, toss the potato with the olive oil, salt, smoked paprika and coriander root. Transfer to a small frying pan, place over medium–high heat and sauté for 15–20 minutes, until golden and crisp.

While the potato is cooking, prepare the tofu scramble. Mash all of the ingredients in a bowl until well combined. Place a frying pan over medium heat, add the mashed tofu and cook, stirring frequently, for 8 minutes or until lightly golden.

Prepare the tomato and jalapeño salsa by placing all of the ingredients in a small bowl and tossing together well. Set aside.

Heat the tortillas according to the packet instructions.

To serve, evenly divide the potato, tofu scramble, tomato and jalapeño salsa, avocado and vegan cheese between the two tortillas. Scatter a few coriander leaves, some sliced jalapeño and pickled red onion over the top, then wrap up into a burrito and serve with lime wedges.

Toddler friendly

Tofu scramble
with spinach & cherry tomatoes

Tofu scramble is one of my favourite breakfasts. As well as being wholesome and filling, it is also extremely versatile. Enjoy it on toast, wrap it in a flour tortilla for a breakfast burrito (see page 55), or save it for lunch to serve as part of a simple nourish bowl.

Serves 2 / gfo (use gf bread)

300 g silken tofu
1 tablespoon olive oil
1 teaspoon vegetable stock powder
1 tablespoon nutritional yeast
¼ teaspoon ground turmeric
150 g (1 cup) cherry tomatoes, halved
45 g (1 cup firmly packed) baby spinach
  leaves

To serve
sourdough toast
mixed herbs, such as flat-leaf parsley and
  sorrel leaves (optional)
freshly ground black pepper

Place the tofu, olive oil, stock powder, nutritional yeast, turmeric and cherry tomatoes in a large bowl. Using a fork, mash the ingredients together until well combined.

Place a large frying pan over high heat, add the tofu mixture and cook, stirring constantly, for about 7 minutes, until lightly golden. Add the spinach and cook, stirring, for another 1½ minutes or until the spinach is wilted. Remove the pan from the heat.

Serve the tofu scramble on toast, topped with some mixed herbs, if desired, and a good grinding of black pepper.

Everyone loves
a toastie!

I think we can all agree that nothing beats a toastie, and here are four of my favourites. They are all packed with flavour and super easy to make! When making toasties, I always recommend using a good-quality sourdough and slicing it yourself to ensure you have nice, thick pieces of bread. Buttering the outside of your bread will also result in a golden colour and amazing crunch.

Tip

I always use a sandwich press for these recipes — it is easy to use, heats up quickly and creates the crispiest toasties. Make sure you preheat your sandwich press before you pop the toastie in for maximum crunch.

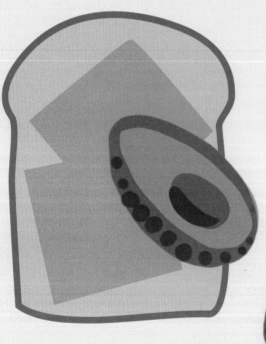

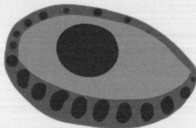

Mushroom, chive & three cheese toastie, see page 62

Baked bean & cheese toastie, see page 69

Avocado, kale & pesto toastie, see page 65

Spicy pepperoni toastie, see page 66

Mushroom, chive
& three cheese toastie

Mushrooms are such a staple vegetable in my household, and they are perfect in this toastie. Accompanied by chives and three different types of vegan cheese, this is packed with flavour and will leave you feeling incredibly satisfied.

Serves 1 / gfo (use gf bread)

1 teaspoon olive oil
3 brown cup mushrooms, cut into 5 mm thick slices
pinch each of sea salt and freshly ground black pepper
vegan butter or olive oil, for spreading
2 slices of sourdough
5 chives, snipped
20 g vegan cheddar cheese, sliced
3 tablespoons grated vegan mature cheddar
1 tablespoon cashew cheese
pinch of dried chilli flakes

Heat the olive oil in a small frying pan over medium–high heat. Add the mushroom, salt and pepper and sauté for 3–4 minutes, until golden and slightly crisp around the edges. Remove the pan from the heat.

Spread the vegan butter or olive oil on one side of the sourdough slices. Top one of the unbuttered sides with the mushroom, chives, cheeses and chilli flakes. Top with the other bread slice, buttered-side up.

Toast in a preheated sandwich press until golden and crisp or cooked to your liking.

Avocado, kale & pesto toastie

In my opinion, you can't go past pesto on a toastie. It is so flavourful and you only need a small amount for it to hit the spot. Accompanied by two of my other favourite ingredients, avocado and kale, this simple toastie is one I make often.

Serves 1 / gfo (use gf bread)

1 tablespoon vegan butter
2 slices of sourdough
1 tablespoon vegan pesto (for a recipe, see page 202)
½ cup finely chopped kale
¼ avocado, sliced
1 slice of vegan cheddar cheese
freshly ground black pepper, to taste
dried chilli flakes, to taste

Spread the vegan butter on one side of the sourdough slices. Top one of the unbuttered sides with the pesto, kale, avocado and cheddar cheese. Season with black pepper and chilli flakes to taste, then top with the other bread slice, buttered-side up.

Toast in a preheated sandwich press until golden and crisp or cooked to your liking.

Spicy pepperoni
toastie

If you love spice, this toastie is for you. The vegan pepperoni and cheese are accompanied by jalapeños, onion and tomato, which makes for a delicious brekkie or lunch.

Serves 1

1 tablespoon vegan butter
2 slices of sourdough
1 tablespoon cashew cheese
1 slice of vegan cheddar cheese
4 slices of tomato
1 slice of whole onion, rings separated
4 slices of vegan spicy pepperoni
3 slices of pickled jalapeño
pinch of freshly ground black pepper

Spread the vegan butter on one side of the sourdough slices. Top one of the unbuttered sides with the cashew cheese, cheddar cheese, tomato, onion, pepperoni, jalapeño and black pepper. Top with the other bread slice, buttered-side up.

Toast in a preheated sandwich press until golden and crisp or cooked to your liking.

Baked bean
& cheese toastie

I love baked beans on toast, but I love them even more in a toastie with cheese. Use leftovers from my cheesy baked beans and enjoy this throughout the week!

Serves 1 / gfo (use gf bread)

1 tablespoon vegan butter
2 slices of sourdough
½ cup leftover Cheesy Baked Beans with
  Roasted Capsicum (see page 79)
3 tablespoons grated vegan cheddar
pinch of freshly ground black pepper

Spread the vegan butter on one side of the sourdough slices. Top one of the unbuttered sides with the leftover baked beans, the cheese and black pepper. Top with the other bread slice, buttered-side up.

Toast in a preheated sandwich press until golden and crisp or cooked to your liking.

Baby/toddler friendly

Hash browns

One of the sides I love to order when I'm out for breakfast is a hash brown – and they are just so easy to make at home, too! My son, Bowie, loves them as much as I do and we enjoy them as a snack or with breakfast.

Makes 8–10 / gfo (use gf flour)

2 large potatoes (about 400 g)
3 tablespoons plain flour
1 teaspoon sea salt flakes
1 tablespoon olive oil, plus extra for frying
1 teaspoon fresh or dried rosemary, plus extra sprigs to serve (optional)
tomato sauce, to serve (optional)

Finely grate the potatoes into a large bowl. Fill the bowl three-quarters full with water and use your hands to wash the grated potato for 1 minute or so. Drain and squeeze any excess liquid from the potato.

Return the potato to the bowl, then sift in the flour and add the salt, olive oil and rosemary. Mix until well combined.

Roll heaped tablespoons of the mixture into balls before flattening them into circles. Repeat until all of the mixture has been used.

Place a large frying pan over medium–high heat and drizzle some olive oil into the pan. Add three or four hash browns and fry for 3 minutes each side until lightly golden, then transfer to a tray. Repeat with the remaining hash browns.

Top with some extra sprigs of rosemary, if you like, and serve the hash browns hot on their own, with tomato sauce, or as a delicious side with breakfast.

Baked tofu & avo
shakshuka

This baked shakshuka is a low-effort and hearty savoury breakfast. I especially love serving it with toasted sourdough and sharing it between two: simply pop the dish in the middle of the table and dunk the bread into the sauce, scooping up bits of tofu and avocado with each bite.

Serves 2 / gfo (use gf bread)

400 g can chopped tomatoes
2 tablespoons finely diced red onion
2 garlic cloves, crushed
¼ teaspoon cayenne pepper (or to taste)
1 teaspoon smoked paprika
½ teaspoon ground cumin
½ teaspoon sea salt
freshly ground black pepper, to taste
150 g soft tofu, cut into 2.5 cm cubes
½ avocado, quartered
2 teaspoons olive oil
2 cubes of marinated vegan feta (for a
  recipe, see page 216)

To serve

1 tablespoon roughly chopped flat-leaf
  parsley leaves
natural coconut yoghurt or cashew cheese
toasted sourdough, flatbread or focaccia

Preheat the oven to 200°C fan-forced.

Place the tomatoes, onion, garlic, spices, salt and pepper in a 20 cm × 15 cm baking dish and stir to combine. Make indents in the tomato mixture and add the tofu. Place the avocado quarters in the gaps among the tofu and press to submerge them in the tomato mixture. Drizzle with the olive oil, mainly coating the avocado. Place or crumble the vegan feta over the top.

Transfer to the oven and bake for 20 minutes or until the sauce is slightly reduced.

Top the shakshuka with the parsley and some coconut yoghurt or cashew cheese. Serve with toasted bread for dipping into the sauce.

Tip

If you don't like the taste of cooked avocado, you can serve it fresh on top after baking.

spicy tomato chickpeas on toast with feta

Chickpeas are such a staple in my diet, and this recipe is the perfect way to use them. Enjoy the heartiness of this breakfast, with the spice of cayenne and sriracha making it extra special.

Serves 4 / gfo (use gf bread)

1 tablespoon olive oil
½ onion, finely diced
2 garlic cloves, crushed
1 teaspoon fennel seeds
½ teaspoon cayenne pepper
1 teaspoon smoked paprika
1 tablespoon sriracha chilli sauce
1 tablespoon coconut sugar
400 g can cherry tomatoes
400 g can chickpeas, rinsed and drained
½ teaspoon sea salt (or to taste)
1 tablespoon freshly squeezed lemon juice

To serve
vegan butter
sourdough toast
vegan feta cubes (for a recipe,
  see page 216)
chopped spring onion
mint leaves
baby sorrel leaves

Heat the olive oil in a saucepan over high heat, then add the onion, garlic, fennel seeds, cayenne pepper and paprika and cook, stirring frequently, for 2–3 minutes. Add the sriracha, coconut sugar, tomatoes and chickpeas and season with the salt. Stir to combine, then cover with a lid, reduce the heat to a simmer and cook, stirring occasionally, for 15 minutes or until slightly reduced and thickened. Remove the pan from the heat and stir in the lemon juice.

Serve the spicy chickpeas on buttered sourdough toast, topped with some cubes of vegan feta, spring onion, mint and sorrel.

Tip

Double the ingredients to make a big batch of spicy chickpeas and keep the leftovers in an airtight container in the fridge for up to 3 days.

cheesy baked beans
with roasted capsicum

Baked beans are such a go-to breakfast for me lately. I love that this dish is filled
with protein and keeps me full for a really long time. It's a great one to make
when you know you have a busy day ahead.

Serves 4 / gfo (use gf bread)

400 g can chopped tomatoes
½ onion, finely chopped
2 garlic cloves, crushed
330 g jar whole roasted red capsicum,
    drained and finely diced
1 teaspoon smoked paprika
1 teaspoon yellow mustard seeds
400 g can cannellini beans, rinsed and
    drained
½ teaspoon red wine vinegar
1 tablespoon olive oil
½ teaspoon sea salt
freshly ground black pepper, to taste
50 g (½ cup) grated vegan cheddar

To serve
toasted sourdough slices
cubed avocado (optional)
roughly chopped flat-leaf parsley leaves
freshly ground black pepper

Preheat the oven to 190°C fan-forced.

Place the tomatoes, onion, garlic, roasted
capsicum, paprika, mustard seeds, cannellini
beans and red wine vinegar in a flameproof
casserole dish. Drizzle with the olive oil and season
with the salt and pepper.

Cover with a lid and bake for 25 minutes, then
uncover and bake for a further 10 minutes. Stir
through the vegan cheddar in the final 5 minutes
of cooking. The beans should be thick and glossy.

Spoon the beans over slices of toasted sourdough.
Scatter over a few cubes of avocado (if desired),
a little parsley and some pepper and serve.

Tip

Keep any leftover
baked beans in an airtight
container in the fridge
for up to 5 days and use
them to make the baked
bean and cheese toastie
on page 69.

Pumpkin soup with crispy sage

Sweetcorn & mushroom soup

Luscious green fennel soup

Shaved broccoli & cranberry salad

Spicy chipotle corn ribs

Bao buns with sticky eggplant

Baked tempeh sticks

Mediterranean chickpea salad

Simple veggie patties

Shaved pear & fennel salad

Lentil bolognese sausage rolls

Pumpkin & broccoli sausage rolls

Spinach & tofu triangles

Sweet potato falafels

Pesto pasta salad with peas & broccolini

Black bean quesadillas with chipotle cream

Air Fryer Recipes

The best crispy potatoes

Salt & pepper tofu with honey—soy dipping sauce

Veggie spring rolls with lettuce & herbs

Crispy lemon pepper cauliflower

Veggie chips, three ways

Crispy curried chickpeas

Sticky maple & sesame eggplant

Light Meals

Pumpkin soup
with crispy sage

A classic pumpkin soup is essential for the cooler seasons. Built on a base of butternut pumpkin and coconut cream, this recipe is very easy to make and great for even the youngest members of the family.

Serves 4 / gfo (use gf bread)

1 tablespoon olive oil or avocado oil
1 onion, finely chopped
3 garlic cloves, crushed
¼ teaspoon ground nutmeg
¼ teaspoon ground cinnamon
2 vegetable stock cubes
900 g butternut pumpkin, peeled and cut
   into 2 cm cubes
½ teaspoon freshly ground black pepper
750 ml (3 cups) boiling water
185 ml (¾ cup) canned coconut cream
dried chilli flakes, to serve (optional)
sliced sourdough, to serve

Crispy sage leaves
2 teaspoons vegan butter
handful of sage leaves

Heat the olive or avocado oil in a large saucepan over high heat. Add the onion and garlic and sauté for 1 minute. Add the nutmeg and cinnamon and sauté for another 30 seconds, then crumble in the vegetable stock cubes, add the pumpkin, black pepper and boiling water. Cover with a lid and bring to the boil, then reduce the heat to a simmer and cook for 12–15 minutes, until the pumpkin is soft.

Transfer the pumpkin mixture to a blender or food processor and blend or process until smooth. Add 125 ml (½ cup) of the coconut cream and blend or process to combine.

To make the crispy sage leaves, melt the vegan butter in a frying pan over high heat. Add the sage leaves and cook for 1–2 minutes, until crisp. Remove the pan from the heat.

Ladle the soup into bowls and drizzle the remaining coconut cream over the top. Top with a couple of sage leaves and a few chilli flakes, if desired. Serve with slices of fresh sourdough bread on the side.

Sweetcorn & mushroom soup

This recipe is so nostalgic for me, as it's something I often used to order when we dined out at restaurants. I figured it was about time I tried making it at home and, oh my goodness, I'm super happy with the results! Perfect as a simple yet hearty dinner, I love making this soup in the cooler months.

Serves 4 / gfo (use tamari instead of soy sauce)

1 tablespoon olive oil
75 g oyster mushrooms, shredded
2.5 cm piece of ginger, finely grated
420 g can creamed sweetcorn
420 g can sweetcorn kernels, rinsed and
  drained
750 ml (3 cups) chicken-style stock
1 tablespoon soy sauce or tamari
sea salt and freshly ground black pepper
300 g silken tofu, mashed with a fork
2 spring onions, finely sliced
1 tablespoon cornflour
1 tablespoon sesame oil
To serve (optional)
chilli powder or dried chilli flakes
sesame seeds
sliced spring onion

Heat the olive oil in a large saucepan over medium heat, add the mushroom and ginger and cook for about 4 minutes, until the mushroom is soft and lightly golden. Add the creamed sweetcorn and sweetcorn kernels, chicken-style stock, soy sauce or tamari and ¼ teaspoon of black pepper, then bring to a simmer, stirring occasionally.

Add the mashed tofu and spring onion to the pan and mix well, then simmer for 1–2 minutes. Reduce the heat to low, then sift in the cornflour, stirring constantly. Add the sesame oil, stir and season with salt and pepper, to taste.

Serve hot, topped with chilli powder or chilli flakes, sesame seeds and sliced spring onion, if desired.

Luscious green
fennel soup

I am passionate about finding new ways to incorporate different vegetables into my diet.
Leek and fennel may not be vegetables you typically see together in the same recipe,
but they work incredibly well in this vibrant soup. If you haven't cooked with these
ingredients before, this is the perfect place to start!

Serves 4–6 / gfo (use gf bread)

1 tablespoon olive oil
2 fennel bulbs, roughly chopped
1 leek, white part only, halved lengthways
  and sliced
3 potatoes, peeled and cut into 2.5 cm cubes
750 ml (3 cups) boiling water
2 vegetable stock cubes
1 head of broccoli, florets roughly chopped
100 g baby spinach leaves
375 ml (1½ cups) soy milk
80 g (½ cup) raw cashews
50 g (½ cup) vegan parmesan (for a recipe,
  see page 216)
sea salt and freshly ground black pepper
2 tablespoons hemp seeds, to serve
crusty baguette or sourdough, to serve

Heat the olive oil in a large saucepan over medium–high heat, then add the fennel and leek, stir well and cover with a lid. Cook for 7 minutes, stirring occasionally, until the vegetables have softened. Add the potato, boiling water and stock cubes, stir well and cover again with the lid. Simmer, stirring occasionally, for another 10 minutes. Stir through the broccoli and simmer, this time uncovered, for 5 minutes.

Ladle half the soup mixture into a blender, along with half the spinach and half the soy milk, and blend until smooth and a rich green colour. Ladle the soup into bowls, then repeat with the remaining soup mixture, spinach and soy milk, but this time also add the cashews and vegan parmesan. Blend again until smooth, then divide among the bowls.

Season with salt and pepper and swirl with a spoon. Top with the hemp seeds and serve with crusty baguette or slices of sourdough.

Shaved broccoli
& cranberry salad

This salad is a great addition to a table spread or for family gatherings such as Christmas Day.
Not only can it be prepared in advance, it also doubles as a delicious main meal.
My tip? Add some canned chickpeas for added protein!

Serves 4 / gf

1 head of broccoli, finely shaved
¼ cup dill fronds, roughly chopped
3 tablespoons dried cranberries
40 g (⅓ cup) pecans, halved lengthways
1 teaspoon finely grated lemon zest
2 teaspoons olive oil
¼ teaspoon sea salt

Dressing
2 garlic cloves, crushed
1 teaspoon wholegrain mustard
2 teaspoons honey (or maple syrup for
  a vegan option)
125 g (½ cup) natural coconut yoghurt
1 tablespoon freshly squeezed lemon juice

Place all of the salad ingredients in a large bowl and toss together.

To make the dressing, place all of the ingredients in a blender and blend until well combined.

Transfer the salad to a large serving bowl or platter and pour the dressing over the top just before serving. Toss well to ensure that everything is evenly coated in the dressing.

Tip

This salad will keep
in an airtight container in
the fridge for 1–2 days.
Feel free to make a big
batch and enjoy the
leftovers the
next day.

Light Meals

Spicy chipotle
corn ribs

I simply could NOT stop eating these corn ribs when I was creating this recipe.
Seriously, they are so good! Enjoy them as a snack or add to a bowl of ramen (see page 170).

Serves 2–4 as a snack / gf

- 2 sweetcorn cobs
- 2 tablespoons vegan butter
- 2 teaspoons chipotle seasoning (or taco seasoning)
- 1 teaspoon smoked paprika
- 1 teaspoon sea salt
- ½ lime

To serve
- 3 tablespoons natural coconut yoghurt
- 1 tablespoon freshly squeezed lime juice
- 1 tablespoon finely chopped coriander leaves

Using a very sharp knife, carefully cut the sweetcorn cobs into quarters lengthways. I find that the easiest way to do this is to stand the corn cobs upright on a chopping board and slowly cut through the middle of each cob. Then cut the halves lengthways in half again.

Mix the vegan butter, spices and salt in a bowl to form a paste. Brush the spiced butter over the corn cobs, reserving one-quarter to brush over the corn ribs as they cook.

Heat a large frying pan over high heat. Add the corn ribs and lime half, flesh-side down, and cook for 2–3 minutes until charred (remove the lime half as soon as it has a little char). Flip the corn ribs over and continue to cook, basting with the leftover spiced butter, for another 2–3 minutes. Finally, flip the corn once more and cook until the kernels are charred and just cooked through.

Meanwhile, mix the coconut yoghurt and lime juice in a small bowl. If it's too thick, add 1 tablespoon of water to loosen it a little.

Transfer the corn ribs to a serving plate, top with the coriander, drizzle with the coconut yoghurt mixture and squeeze over the juice of the charred lime.

Bao buns
with sticky eggplant

Bao have always been one of my favourite things to order when I'm dining out, so I decided it was time to make them in the comfort of my own home. Super simple and great for sharing, this recipe calls for my sticky maple and sesame eggplant, but this can be substituted for salt and pepper tofu (see page 127) or lemon pepper cauliflower (see page 130) if you like.

Makes 8–10

1 × quantity Sticky Maple and Sesame
  Eggplant (see page 138)
8–10 fluffy bao buns (see Tip)
1 head of baby cos lettuce, leaves separated
1 Lebanese cucumber, cut into matchsticks
1 carrot, cut into matchsticks

To serve
vegan Kewpie mayo
finely sliced spring onion
toasted sesame seeds

First, prepare the sticky maple and sesame eggplant. Steam the bao buns according to the packet instructions, then set aside until cool enough to handle.

Now all you need to do is assemble your bao. To do this, fill each bao with 1–2 small leaves of cos lettuce, 3–4 matchsticks each of cucumber and carrot and 3–4 pieces of sticky eggplant.

Transfer the bao buns to a platter or individual plates, then top with a little vegan mayo, spring onion and sesame seeds. Serve while hot.

Tip

Look for fresh bao buns at your local Asian grocer. You can also buy them frozen, which means you'll always have delicious bao on hand!

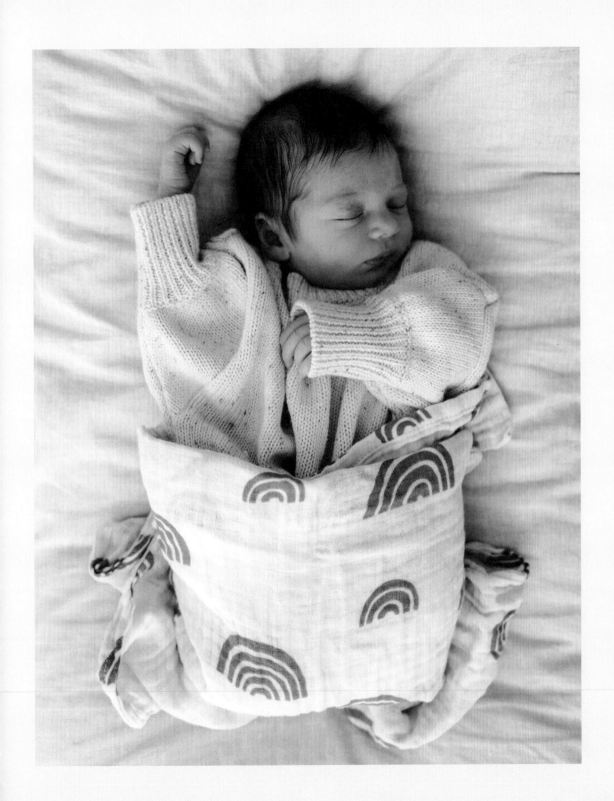

Toddler friendly

Baked
tempeh sticks

I like to make these baked tempeh sticks to enjoy throughout the week.
They are perfect as a delicious afternoon snack, in a toasted sandwich
or as a great protein source in a salad.

Serves 4

300 g tempeh, cut into 1 cm thick slices
1 tablespoon tamari
1 tablespoon teriyaki sauce
1 tablespoon sesame oil
pinch of freshly ground black pepper
To serve (optional)
salt flakes and freshly ground black pepper
roughly chopped flat-leaf parsley leaves

Preheat the oven to 180°C fan-forced. Line a
baking tray with baking paper.

Meanwhile, place the ingredients in a non-reactive
container, then seal and shake well to coat the
tempeh. Leave to marinate for 15 minutes while
the oven heats up.

Place the tempeh on the prepared tray, evenly
spaced apart, and bake for 20 minutes or until
crisp and golden.

You can enjoy these on their own or, if you like,
sprinkle with some salt, pepper and chopped
parsley leaves.

The baked tempeh will keep in an airtight
container in the fridge for up to 5 days.

Tip

Serve these
tempeh sticks with
vegan chipotle mayo
for an extra kick
of flavour.

Mediterranean
chickpea salad

I love making this chickpea salad for a super quick, simple and fresh lunch that's perfect for a summer's day! Packed with flavour and protein and coated with a delicious dressing, it's sure to become a favourite of yours, too.

Serves 2 / gf

400 g can chickpeas, rinsed and drained
1 Lebanese cucumber, chopped into
   2.5 cm pieces
¼ red onion, finely diced
230 g jar pitted Sicilian olives, drained
60 g vegan feta (for a recipe, see
   page 216), crumbled
250 g punnet of cherry tomatoes, halved
   or quartered
¼ teaspoon sea salt
freshly ground black pepper, to taste
handful of flat-leaf parsley leaves,
   roughly chopped
½ teaspoon dried chilli flakes
finely grated zest and juice of ½ lemon
1 tablespoon olive oil
1 teaspoon white wine vinegar

This one is incredibly simple – just add all of the ingredients to a large salad bowl and toss together well.

Serve immediately and enjoy! The salad will keep in an airtight container in the fridge for up to 3 days.

Tip

Prepare a double
batch of this salad
on the weekend to enjoy
as a quick and easy
lunch throughout
the week!

Simple
veggie patties

These veggie patties are so versatile! Not only are they baby and toddler friendly, they are a delicious snack for adults or the perfect addition to a salad or burger. Packed with vegetables and flavour, they are sure to be a hit with the whole family.

Makes 14–18 / gf

400 g potato, peeled and chopped into 2 cm pieces
230 g (2 cups) frozen mixed veg (peas, corn and carrots)
1 tablespoon dill fronds, finely chopped
400 g can chickpeas, drained, rinsed and mashed
½–2 teaspoons sea salt (½–1 teaspoon for babies)
50 g (⅓ cup) gluten-free flour (see Tip, page 114)
2 tablespoons hemp seeds
1 tablespoon olive oil
2 tablespoons freshly squeezed lemon juice
30 g (½ cup) dried gluten-free breadcrumbs

To serve (optional)
natural coconut yoghurt or Cheat's Sour Cream (see page 201)
roughly chopped herbs
lemon wedges

Preheat the oven to 180°C fan-forced. Line a large baking tray with baking paper.

Bring a large saucepan of water to the boil, add the potato and boil for 15–20 minutes, until soft. Add the frozen mixed veg to the pan in the last 2 minutes of cooking to soften.

Drain the vegetables, then transfer to a large mixing bowl and add the dill, mashed chickpeas, salt, flour, hemp seeds, olive oil and lemon juice, and mix until well combined.

Pour the breadcrumbs into a shallow bowl. Use your hands to mould the veggie mixture into patties about 8–10 cm wide and 1–2 cm high. Toss each patty in the breadcrumbs, then transfer to the prepared tray.

Bake the veggie patties for 30 minutes or until lightly golden. Serve warm on their own or, if you like, with coconut yoghurt or cheat's sour cream, chopped herbs and lemon wedges.

Leftover patties will keep in an airtight container in the fridge for up to 5 days. You can also freeze them for up to 2 weeks. Simply bake from frozen until cooked through and golden.

Shaved pear
& fennel salad

This unique salad is quick and simple to put together. The pear adds a sweetness
to the dish, which is balanced by the bite of the fennel. Enjoy this on its own, as a side salad
or with a hearty dinner such as the roasted cauliflower steaks on page 148.

Serves 4 / gf

1 pear, shaved using a mandoline
1 fennel bulb, shaved using a mandoline
3 tablespoons finely chopped dill fronds
3 tablespoons hemp seeds
1 tablespoon olive oil
1 tablespoon white wine vinegar
½ teaspoon sea salt
freshly ground black pepper, to taste
large handful of walnuts, roughly chopped

Place all of the ingredients except the walnuts in
a large bowl and toss together well.

Transfer to a serving plate or bowl, top with the
walnuts and serve straight away.

Vegan pastries, three ways

Pies, sausage rolls and pasties are such classic party foods here in Australia. These plant-based pastry recipes are packed full of flavour and guarantee that there's something for everyone. Take them to a picnic or serve them at your next barbecue or gathering.

I have included three different variations here – spinach and tofu triangles, lentil bolognese sausage rolls, and pumpkin and broccoli sausage rolls. All three are delicious served with a classic tomato sauce.

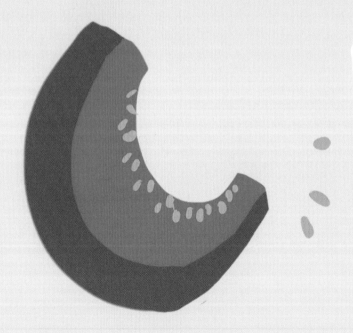

Tip

These pastries can be frozen, uncooked, in an airtight container for up to 3 months. To cook, preheat the oven to 180°C fan-forced and bake from frozen for 30–40 minutes until golden and crisp.

Spinach & tofu triangles,
see page 113

Lentil bolognese
sausage rolls,
see page 111

Pumpkin & broccoli
sausage rolls,
see page 112

lentil bolognese
sausage rolls

These lentil sausage rolls are perfect for a picnic on a summer's day and will be devoured by both kids and adults.

Serves 4

3 tablespoons olive oil
½ onion, finely diced
1 celery stalk, finely diced
1 carrot, finely diced
1 tablespoon finely chopped oregano leaves
400 g can lentils, rinsed and drained
210 g canned chopped tomatoes
40 g (⅓ cup) crushed walnuts
½ teaspoon sea salt
½ teaspoon freshly ground black pepper
2 vegan puff pastry sheets, thawed
black sesame seeds, for sprinkling (optional)
your choice of dipping sauce, to serve

Preheat the oven to 180°C fan-forced. Line a baking tray with baking paper.

Heat the olive oil in a frying pan over medium heat. Add the onion, celery, carrot and oregano and cook for 3 minutes or until the onion is translucent. Add the lentils, tomatoes, walnuts, salt and pepper and cook for 3 minutes or until slightly reduced and thickened. Remove the pan from the heat and set aside to cool.

Place the pastry sheets in front of you and spoon the filling along the edge of each pastry sheet that's closest to you leaving a 2 cm border. Gently shape the filling into a sausage, then, working with one pastry sheet at a time, fold the pastry over the filling and roll it up into a large sausage roll. Top with a few sesame seeds, if desired, then cut the sausage rolls into lengths of your choice.

Transfer to the prepared tray and bake for 20–25 minutes, until the pastry is puffed up and golden. Allow the sausage rolls to cool slightly and serve warm with your choice of sauce.

Pumpkin & broccoli sausage rolls

These pumpkin rolls are absolutely delicious and packed with veggies to keep you feeling nourished. Top with pumpkin seeds for extra colour and crunch!

Serves 4

600 g pumpkin (any variety is fine), peeled and roughly chopped
1 head of broccoli, finely chopped or grated
½ teaspoon sea salt
½ teaspoon freshly ground black pepper
1 tablespoon olive oil
30 g (¼ cup) pumpkin seeds, plus extra for sprinkling (optional)
2 vegan puff pastry sheets, thawed
your choice of dipping sauce, to serve

Caramelised onion

1 tablespoon olive oil
1 onion, finely sliced
1 tablespoon brown sugar
½ teaspoon sea salt

Preheat the oven to 180°C fan-forced. Line a baking tray with baking paper.

Bring a saucepan of water to the boil over high heat. Add the pumpkin and boil for about 10 minutes or until soft.

Meanwhile, place the broccoli, salt, pepper, olive oil and pumpkin seeds in a large bowl.

To make the caramelised onion, heat the olive oil in a small frying pan over medium–high heat, add the onion, sugar and salt and cook for 5–8 minutes, until caramelised.

Drain the pumpkin and add it to the broccoli mixture. Using a fork, mash the pumpkin into the broccoli mixture until well combined. Add the caramelised onion and stir through to combine.

Cut each pastry sheet into four squares. Divide the filling among the squares, placing it in a central strip from one diagonal corner to another. Fold the two remaining corners over the filling to meet in the middle, then top with a few extra pumpkin seeds, if desired.

Transfer to the prepared tray and bake for 20–25 minutes, until the pastry is puffed up and golden. Allow the rolls to cool slightly and serve warm with your choice of sauce.

spinach & tofu
triangles

These spinach and tofu triangles are my favourite pastry in this book! Trust me, you have to try them. The filling is creamy and delicious, as well as being rich in protein from the cashews and tofu.

Serves 4

155 g (1 cup) raw cashews
250 g frozen spinach, thawed
250 g firm tofu, crumbled
1 tablespoon finely grated lemon zest
1 small onion, finely diced
3 tablespoons olive oil
80 ml (⅓ cup) freshly squeezed lemon juice
20 g (⅓ cup) nutritional yeast
1 teaspoon sea salt
1 teaspoon freshly ground black pepper
2 vegan puff pastry sheets, thawed
fennel seeds, for sprinkling (optional)
your choice of dipping sauce, to serve

Preheat the oven to 180°C fan-forced. Line a baking tray with baking paper.

Place the cashews in a bowl, cover with boiling water and allow to soak for 5 minutes.

Place the spinach, tofu, lemon zest and onion in a large bowl and mix well to combine.

Drain the cashews and add them to a blender with the olive oil, lemon juice, nutritional yeast, salt, pepper and 3 tablespoons of water. Blend until smooth, adding a little more water if needed to get the mixture moving. Add the cashew mixture to the spinach and tofu mixture and stir through.

Cut the pastry sheets in half so you have four rectangles. Place the pastry sheets vertically in front of you, then place one-quarter of the filling at the base of each rectangle. Working with one pastry sheet at a time, fold the end of the pastry over the filling to form a triangle, then continue to fold it over in a triangle shape until you reach the end of the pastry. Press the sides to seal in the filling if necessary.

Top with a few fennel seeds, if desired, then transfer to the prepared tray and bake for 20–25 minutes, until the pastry is puffed up and golden. Allow the sausage rolls to cool slightly and serve warm with your choice of sauce.

Sweet potato falafels

Falafels are a great staple to have in the fridge, and I love them even more when they're homemade. Enjoy these with a colourful salad, in a wrap or simply dipped in hummus.

Makes 18–20 / gf

500 g sweet potato, peeled and cut into
  2.5 cm pieces
2 × 400 g cans chickpeas, rinsed and drained
2 teaspoons ground cumin
1 garlic clove, crushed
1 long red chilli, chopped
1 teaspoon sea salt
⅓ cup coriander leaves, chopped
½ teaspoon ground turmeric
1 tablespoon olive oil
250 g (1½ cups) gluten-free flour (see Tip)
135 g (½ cup) hulled tahini
black and white sesame seeds, for coating
  (optional)
olive oil spray (optional)
To serve (optional)
hummus
salad of your choice
sriracha chilli sauce
pita bread
lemon wedges
Pickled Red Onion (see page 227)

Preheat the oven to 180°C fan-forced. Line a baking tray with baking paper.

Bring a large saucepan of water to the boil over high heat, add the sweet potato and boil for 20 minutes or until soft. Drain, then transfer to a food processor. Add the chickpeas, cumin, garlic, chilli, salt, coriander, turmeric, olive oil, flour and tahini and blend until smooth.

Transfer the falafel mixture to a large bowl. Sprinkle the sesame seeds (if using) onto a flat plate. Using wet hands, roll heaped tablespoon-sized portions of the falafel mixture into balls, then roll in the sesame seeds to coat. Place on the prepared tray and spray with olive oil, if desired. Transfer to the oven and bake for 30 minutes or until golden and slightly crisp.

Serve the falafels on their own with some hummus or with your favourite salad, sriracha, pita bread, lemon wedges and pickled red onion.

Any leftover falafels will keep in an airtight container in the fridge for up to 3 days. Alternatively, freeze the uncooked falafels for up to 3 months. Cook from frozen and increase the baking time to 35–40 minutes.

Tip

I recommend Orgran brand gluten-free flour.

Pesto pasta salad
with peas & broccolini

This simple pasta salad is packed full of delicious green veggies making it a perfect lunch for the whole family to enjoy (or if you want to keep it all for yourself and enjoy it throughout the week, I wouldn't blame you!).

Serves 4 / gfo (use gf pasta)

400 g rigatoni pasta
310 g (2 cups) frozen peas
1 tablespoon olive oil
150 g broccolini, trimmed
1 × quantity Speedy Cashew Pesto
   (see page 202)
90 g (½ cup) pitted green olives, sliced
small handful of dill fronds, roughly chopped
lemon halves, to serve

Bring a large saucepan of salted water to the boil and cook the pasta according to the packet instructions until al dente. Drain well and place in a large bowl.

Run the peas under hot water to thaw.

Heat the olive oil in a large frying pan over medium–high heat. Add the broccolini and cook for 1½ minutes, then turn over and cook for another minute. Transfer to a plate.

Add the pesto to the bowl with the pasta and mix through. Add the peas, olives, broccolini and dill and toss everything together. Serve at room temperature with lemon halves for squeezing over.

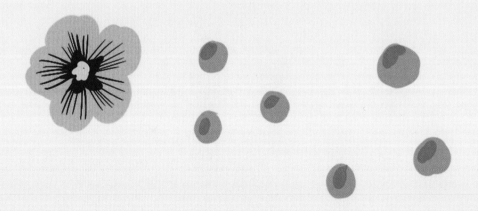

Light Meals

Black bean quesadillas
with chipotle cream

Quesadillas are not only a hit with me, but also with my toddler. I love adding vegetables and black beans for some hidden extra nutrients. If you are making these for adults rather than kids, you can add some spice, such as cayenne pepper and fresh jalapeños.

Makes 5 / gfo (use gf tortillas)

1 tablespoon olive oil
½ red capsicum, very finely sliced
1 sweetcorn cob, kernels stripped
½ zucchini, finely sliced
½ teaspoon smoked paprika
¼ teaspoon sea salt
10 mini flour tortillas
100 g (½ cup) canned black beans, rinsed and drained
40 g (1 cup) grated vegan cheese (see Tips)

Chipotle cream
125 g (½ cup) natural coconut yoghurt
1 tablespoon chipotle sauce
1 teaspoon freshly squeezed lime juice

To serve (optional)
guacamole (for a recipe, see page 214)
sliced fresh jalapeño
lime wedges
Pickled Red Onion (see page 227)

Tips

If you don't have a sandwich press, you can make these in a large frying pan — simply cook over medium heat for 2—3 minutes each side until golden. You can also bake them in a preheated 180°C oven for 5—10 minutes.

My favourite brand of grated vegan cheese is Sheese.

Heat a non-stick frying pan over medium heat. Add the olive oil, capsicum, sweetcorn and zucchini and fry for 1 minute. Add the paprika and salt and continue to fry, stirring, for a further 3 minutes or until the veggies are soft and slightly charred. Remove the pan from the heat.

Preheat a sandwich press.

Lay out five tortillas and top each with one-fifth of the veggie mix. Add a heaped tablespoon of the black beans and evenly sprinkle over the vegan cheese. Place the remaining tortillas on top, then transfer one (or two if they will fit) to the sandwich press and close. Toast for 4 minutes or until golden. Transfer to a wooden board and repeat with the remaining quesadillas.

While the quesadillas are cooking, prepare the chipotle cream by combining the yoghurt, chipotle sauce and lime juice in a small bowl.

Cut the quesadillas into quarters and serve with the chipotle cream. If you like, you can also serve with your choice of guacamole, sliced jalapeño, lime wedges and pickled red onion.

Air Fryer Recipes

Toddler friendly

The best
crispy potatoes

Everyone loves crispy potatoes, right? If not, I hope this recipe changes your mind.
Rosemary and breadcrumbs add flavour and crunch to these air-fried potatoes.
They are perfect to share with friends for a Sunday lunch, served with my cauliflower steaks
(see page 148) and pear and fennel salad (see page 105).

Serves 4 / gfo (use gf breadcrumbs)

700 g potatoes, scrubbed and cut into
    2 cm pieces
1 tablespoon olive oil
1 teaspoon vegetable stock powder
1 sprig of rosemary, leaves picked
2 tablespoons dried breadcrumbs

To serve
sea salt
tomato sauce
mustard of your choice

Place the potato, olive oil, vegetable stock powder, rosemary leaves and breadcrumbs in a bowl and toss together.

Transfer the potato mixture to your air fryer and cook at 200°C on the vegetable setting for 25 minutes or until golden and crispy.

Sprinkle the crispy potatoes with sea salt and serve with tomato sauce and your favourite mustard.

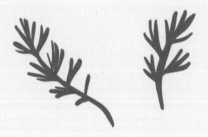

Salt & pepper tofu
with honey–soy dipping sauce

Salt and pepper tofu is such a classic dish, and I always order it if it's on the menu when I eat out. I wanted to make a healthier version at home, so I created this air fryer recipe which works really well. It's super quick and easy to prepare, and makes a great starter or snack to share with friends.

Serves 4 / gfo (use tamari instead of soy sauce)

2 tablespoons cornflour
¼ teaspoon sea salt
¼ teaspoon freshly ground black pepper
1 teaspoon onion powder
300 g firm tofu, cut into 2 cm cubes
2 teaspoons olive oil

Honey–soy dipping sauce

1 tablespoon soy sauce
1 tablespoon honey (or maple syrup for a vegan option)
1 long red chilli, finely chopped
1 spring onion, finely sliced
1 tablespoon finely chopped coriander leaves and stalks

To serve

sliced long red chilli
sliced spring onion
dill fronds
black and white sesame seeds
lime wedges

Preheat your air fryer to 200°C on the vegetable setting.

Combine the cornflour, salt, pepper and onion powder in a shallow bowl. Add the tofu and toss to coat in the cornflour mixture, then transfer to the air fryer. Drizzle the olive oil over the tofu, then cook for 15 minutes or until golden and crispy.

Meanwhile, to make the honey–soy dipping sauce, combine all of the ingredients in a small bowl.

Transfer the salt and pepper tofu to a serving plate and scatter the sliced chilli, spring onion, dill and sesame seeds over the top. Serve immediately with lime wedges and the dipping sauce.

Veggie spring rolls
with lettuce & herbs

These homemade spring rolls are the real deal. Packed full of veggies and tofu,
they are flavoursome, nourishing and make the ultimate party snack.
Wrap them in lettuce and serve with herbs for extra freshness in each bite.

Makes 12–14

100 g mixed mushrooms, finely diced
¼ green cabbage, shredded
1 carrot, shredded or julienned
300 g firm tofu, crumbled
2 garlic cloves, crushed
½ teaspoon Chinese five spice
1 teaspoon sea salt
½ teaspoon freshly ground black pepper
1 tablespoon sesame oil
12–14 spring roll sheets
olive oil spray (optional)

Dipping sauce
1 teaspoon rice wine vinegar
1 teaspoon sesame oil
1 tablespoon soy sauce
juice of ½ lime (about 1 tablespoon)

To serve
cos lettuce leaves
Thai basil, coriander, dill and mint leaves
sliced long red chilli
lime wedges
sesame seeds

Preheat your air fryer to 200°C on the vegetable setting. Line a baking tray with baking paper. Alternatively, preheat the oven to 220°C fan-forced.

Combine the mushroom, cabbage, carrot and tofu in a large bowl. Add the garlic, Chinese five spice, salt, pepper and sesame oil and mix well to combine.

Spoon about 3 tablespoons of the mixture onto each spring roll sheet. Roll into spring rolls, tucking in the ends as you roll, then place on the prepared tray or directly in the air fryer. Spray the spring rolls with olive oil spray, if desired.

Cook the spring rolls in the air fryer for 15 minutes until golden and crisp. If using the oven, bake for 10 minutes, then turn them over and bake for a further 9 minutes.

Meanwhile, to make the dipping sauce, combine all of the ingredients in a small bowl.

Place the spring rolls on a serving platter along with some cos lettuce leaves, herbs, sliced red chilli, lime wedges and a sprinkle of sesame seeds. To serve, place a spring roll, a few herbs and chilli slices in a lettuce leaf and wrap it up. Drizzle with or dip into the dipping sauce and enjoy.

crispy lemon pepper
cauliflower

This has to be the crispiest cauliflower I've ever eaten. It perfectly combines sweet and savoury flavours, and pairs really well with my cheat's sour cream. Serve as a snack or starter, or as part of a shared feast.

Serves 2 / gfo (use gf flour and breadcrumbs)

75 g (½ cup) plain flour
185 ml (¾ cup) soy milk
2 teaspoons lemon pepper seasoning
finely grated zest of 1 lemon
100 g (1 cup) dried breadcrumbs
½ head of cauliflower, chopped into florets

Glaze
1 tablespoon honey (or maple syrup for
  a vegan option)
juice of ¼ lemon
2 teaspoons olive oil
1 teaspoon lemon pepper seasoning

To serve
Cheat's Sour Cream (see page 201)
sweet chilli sauce
chopped flat-leaf parsley leaves
freshly ground black pepper
lemon wedges

Preheat your air fryer to 200°C on the vegetable setting.

Whisk together the flour, milk, lemon pepper seasoning and half the lemon zest in a bowl to make a batter.

Mix the breadcrumbs and the remaining lemon zest in another bowl.

Dunk the cauliflower florets in the batter and then coat them in the lemony breadcrumbs. Transfer the cauliflower to the air fryer and cook for 20 minutes or until golden and crisp.

While the cauliflower is cooking, make the glaze by combining the honey, lemon juice, olive oil and lemon pepper seasoning in a small bowl.

Remove the crispy cauliflower from the air fryer and generously brush with the glaze, then return to the air fryer and cook for another 5 minutes.

Spoon the cheat's sour cream into a bowl and swirl through a little sweet chilli sauce.

Transfer the cauliflower to a platter, scatter a little parsley and black pepper over the top and serve hot with the sour cream and lemon wedges.

Toddler friendly

Veggie chips, three ways

I'm not joking when I say an air fryer is absolutely *game-changing*. These veggie chips are SO quick and easy to make with an air fryer, you'll find yourself whipping them up for visitors frequently. With potato, sweet potato and carrot, there's something to please everyone. Use my vegan parmesan in this recipe for extra deliciousness!

Serves 4 / gf

2 potatoes (about 480 g), scrubbed
2 small carrots (about 120 g), scrubbed
1 small or ½ large sweet potato
  (about 370 g), scrubbed
2 teaspoons sea salt
2 tablespoons olive oil
2 tablespoons vegan parmesan (for a recipe,
  see page 216)
1 teaspoon onion powder
1 teaspoon dried thyme

To serve
soft herbs of your choice (optional)
vegan mayonnaise
lemon wedges

Cut the potatoes, carrots and sweet potato into thin chips. Place in a large bowl and add the salt, olive oil, vegan parmesan, onion powder and dried thyme. Toss together well.

Transfer the chips to your air fryer and cook at 200°C on the vegetable setting for 15 minutes or until golden and crispy.

Scatter some herbs over the veggie chips, if you like, and serve hot with a bowl of vegan mayonnaise and lemon wedges.

Crispy curried
chickpeas

I love making these crispy chickpeas to enjoy as a snack or in a hearty salad bowl. The air fryer makes this dish even quicker and easier to prepare, while the addition of curry powder adds a burst of flavour.

Makes 400 g / gf

400 g can chickpeas, rinsed and drained
1 teaspoon olive oil
1 teaspoon curry powder
¼ teaspoon sea salt

Preheat your air fryer to 200°C on the vegetable setting.

Place the chickpeas, olive oil, curry powder and salt in a bowl and toss together until the chickpeas are well coated.

Transfer the chickpeas to the air fryer and cook for 15 minutes or until golden and crispy.

Remove the chickpeas from the air fryer, transfer to a serving bowl and enjoy on their own or in a delicious salad or wrap.

Any leftovers will keep in an airtight container in the fridge for 3 days.

Tip

Try mixing up the flavour of these crispy chickpeas by swapping the curry powder for other spices, such as ground cumin, smoked paprika and garlic powder, or even some dried Italian herbs for something different!

Sticky maple
& sesame eggplant

Sticky eggplant just got even easier by using an air fryer! With a deliciously sweet glaze
and quick cooking time, this dish is an absolute hit with my family and friends.
Perfect as a starter for everyone to share.

*Serves 4 / gfo (use tamari instead of soy
sauce and gf noodles or rice)*

80 ml (⅓ cup) maple syrup
1 tablespoon tamari
1 tablespoon sesame oil
1 teaspoon red miso paste
1 tablespoon sesame seeds
2 teaspoons apple cider vinegar
1 large or 2 small eggplants (about 700 g),
   chopped into 5 cm pieces

Sticky eggplant glaze
3 tablespoons maple syrup
1 tablespoon soy sauce

To serve
cooked rice or noodles of your choice
sliced spring onion
sesame seeds

Preheat your air fryer to 200°C on the vegetable
setting.

Combine the maple syrup, tamari, sesame oil, red
miso paste, sesame seeds and apple cider vinegar
in a bowl. Place the eggplant in the air fryer and
pour the sauce over the top to coat, then cook for
20 minutes.

While the eggplant is cooking, prepare the sticky
glaze by mixing the ingredients in a small bowl.

Once the eggplant is cooked, transfer it to a
serving bowl. Drizzle the glaze over the top, then
top with sliced spring onion and sesame seeds and
serve with rice or noodles.

Slow Cooker Recipes

Mains

Baby/toddler friendly

Bowie's simple
lentils

Super simple and filled with flavour, these lentils are sure to become a staple meal in your week. You can finely grate and add any veggies to this dish to encourage your baby to try new flavours and textures, or simply to use up what's in the fridge!

Serves 2 / gfo (use gf pasta)

400 g can lentils, rinsed and drained
400 g can chopped tomatoes
1 carrot, finely grated
3 broccoli florets and stalks, finely grated
¼ teaspoon ground cinnamon
½ teaspoon dried basil
sea salt and freshly ground black pepper,
  to taste

To serve (optional)
natural coconut yoghurt
diced avocado
mashed potato
cooked pasta

Toppings (optional)
nutritional yeast
finely snipped chives
finely chopped flat-leaf parsley leaves
hemp seeds

Place all of the ingredients in a large saucepan and stir to combine. Place over high heat and bring to the boil, then reduce the heat to a simmer and cook, uncovered, for 5 minutes or until slightly reduced.

Serve the lentils warm with your choice of coconut yoghurt, avocado, mashed potato or pasta. Scatter over whichever toppings you like and serve.

Tips

Double the quantities if you're making this for a family of four.

If making this for your baby, divide any leftovers into individual portions and store in the freezer for up to 1 month.

Smoky cauliflower steaks with salsa verde

If you haven't tried cauliflower steaks yet, this recipe is a great place to start.
Paired with my crispy potatoes and pear and fennel salad, it makes the perfect Sunday lunch
to share with friends or family. The salsa verde adds a wonderful zing to the finished dish.

Serves 2–3 / gf

½ teaspoon dried chilli flakes
1 teaspoon dried parsley or oregano
1 teaspoon smoked paprika
½ teaspoon garlic powder
½ teaspoon sea salt
½ teaspoon freshly ground black pepper
1 head of cauliflower
1 tablespoon olive oil

To serve
Zesty Salsa Verde (see page 211)
Shaved Pear and Fennel Salad (see page 105)
The Best Crispy Potatoes (see page 124)

Preheat the oven to 200°C fan-forced. Line a baking tray with baking paper.

Combine the chilli flakes, parsley or oregano, smoked paprika, garlic powder, salt and pepper in a small bowl.

Cut the cauliflower lengthways through the core into 2–3 cm thick slices – you should get about three steaks from a whole cauliflower, and you can either bake the remaining cauliflower pieces or transfer them to an airtight container and place in the fridge to save for other recipes.

Lay the cauliflower steaks on the prepared tray and brush with half the olive oil. Sprinkle with about half the chilli seasoning, then transfer to the oven and bake for 15 minutes.

Remove the tray from the oven, flip the steaks over and brush with the remaining olive oil. Sprinkle with the remaining chilli seasoning, then return to the oven for another 15 minutes or until golden and cooked through.

Drizzle the cauliflower steaks with some salsa verde and serve with my pear and fennel salad and crispy potatoes.

crispy teriyaki tofu bowl

The cornflour coating in this recipe makes for a delicious crispy tofu that pairs perfectly with the freshness of the veggies. The teriyaki sauce adds an earthy splash of flavour, while the Japanese seasoning, shichimi togarashi, adds a subtle spicy kick.

I use a julienne peeler to slice the carrot into super thin strips – it's easy to use and so much faster than julienning with a knife.

Serves 2

220 g (1 cup) white rice
250 g silken tofu
3 tablespoons cornflour
¼ teaspoon sea salt
pinch of freshly ground black pepper
1 tablespoon olive oil
1 carrot, julienned
75 g (1 cup) shredded red cabbage
1 avocado, diced
1 spring onion, finely sliced
2 teaspoons sesame seeds
1 teaspoon shichimi togarashi (see Tip)
3 tablespoons teriyaki sauce

Rinse the rice under cold running water, massaging it well with your hands. Transfer to a rice cooker or saucepan and cook according to the packet instructions.

Using paper towel, very gently press the tofu to remove the excess moisture, then cut the tofu into 2.5 cm cubes. Combine the cornflour, salt and pepper in a small bowl.

Heat the olive oil in a frying pan over medium–high heat. Gently roll the tofu in the cornflour mixture, then transfer to the pan and cook, turning, for 2 minutes or until golden on all sides.

Divide the rice among bowls and add the carrot, cabbage, avocado, spring onion, sesame seeds and crispy tofu. Sprinkle the shichimi togarashi over the top and finish by drizzling with the teriyaki sauce.

Tip

Shichimi togarashi is a Japanese dried spice blend. You can purchase it from Asian grocers and some supermarkets.

Lentil
shepherd's pie

Who doesn't love a good shepherd's pie? This plant-based alternative is one of my all-time favourite winter recipes. It's so hearty, packed full of veggies and heavy on the protein with a couple of cans of lentils.

Serves 4–6 / gf

1 tablespoon olive oil
2 × 400 g cans lentils, rinsed and drained
465 g (3 cups) frozen mixed veg (peas, corn and carrots)
400 g can chopped tomatoes
3 tablespoons onion gravy powder
2 teaspoons dried thyme
3 tablespoons vegan red wine
sea salt and freshly ground black pepper
chopped flat-leaf parsley leaves, to serve

Potato topping
540 g potatoes, peeled and cut into 2.5 cm chunks
2 tablespoons vegan butter
3 tablespoons soy milk
¼ teaspoon sea salt
2 teaspoons dried parsley, plus extra for sprinkling

Preheat the oven to 180°C fan-forced.

Start with the potato topping. Bring a large saucepan of water to the boil, add the potato, cover and boil for 10–15 minutes, until soft. Drain and return the potato to the pan, then add the butter, soy milk, salt and dried parsley. Mash until smooth and fluffy. Set aside.

Heat the olive oil in a large saucepan over medium–high heat. Add the lentils, frozen mixed veg, tomatoes, gravy powder and thyme. Stir and bring to a simmer, then cook for 5 minutes. Stir through the red wine and continue to simmer for 3 minutes, then season with salt and pepper to taste.

Transfer the lentil and vegetable mixture to a large baking dish and evenly spread the mashed potato over the top. Sprinkle with a little extra dried parsley, then transfer to the oven and bake for 25 minutes or until the potato is golden and crisp.

Scatter some chopped parsley over the shepherd's pie and serve hot.

Sweet & spicy
cauliflower salad

**Hearty, zesty, tasty and wholesome – everything you want in a salad!
The hero of this salad is the warm baked cauliflower on top; it's sweet, salty
and spicy, and brings all of the ingredients together.**

Serves 3–4 / gf

200 g (1 cup) tri-colour quinoa, rinsed
1 sweetcorn cob, kernels stripped
400 g can black beans, rinsed and drained
150 g (1 cup) cherry tomatoes, quartered
½ cup vegan feta cubes (for a recipe, see
  page 216)
handful of coriander leaves

Sweet & spicy cauliflower
300 g cauliflower, cut into small florets
1 teaspoon smoked paprika
1 teaspoon ground cumin
2 teaspoons olive oil
½ teaspoon sea salt
1 tablespoon honey (or maple syrup for
  a vegan option)

Coriander dressing
large handful (14 g) of coriander leaves
  and stalks
3 tablespoons olive oil
1 tablespoon red wine vinegar
½ teaspoon sea salt
freshly ground black pepper, to taste
juice of ½ lemon

Preheat the oven to 200°C fan-forced. Line a baking tray with baking paper.

Place the quinoa and 500 ml (2 cups) of water in a saucepan over medium heat. Cover and cook for 10–15 minutes, until the liquid is absorbed and the quinoa is cooked through. Add the sweetcorn kernels in the last minute of cooking, to soften. Transfer to a large salad bowl and allow to cool.

Meanwhile, to make the sweet and spicy cauliflower, place all of the ingredients in a large bowl, tossing to evenly coat the cauliflower. Transfer to the prepared tray and roast for 25 minutes or until the cauliflower is really crispy at the edges.

To make the coriander dressing, place all of the ingredients in a food processor or blender and process or blend for 30 seconds or until you have a smooth sauce. If you don't have a food processor or blender, you can finely chop the coriander and add it to a bowl with the remaining ingredients, whisking to combine.

Pour the coriander dressing over the quinoa and sweetcorn and stir to combine, then add the black beans and cherry tomatoes and toss well. Scatter the roasted cauliflower, vegan feta and coriander leaves over the salad and serve straight away.

Mac
& greens

If you've enjoyed my mac-no-cheese, it's time to try my mac and greens!
This creamy pasta sauce features spinach and peas to get those greens in, while the
addition of pan-fried broccoli adds another dimension – I can't get enough of it.

Serves 4 / gfo (use gf pasta)

250 g cauliflower, florets roughly chopped
155 g (1 cup) raw cashews
½ teaspoon sea salt
500 g pasta elbows
155 g (1 cup) frozen peas
2 tablespoons olive oil
1 small head of broccoli, florets roughly
  chopped
125 ml (½ cup) soy milk
30 g (½ cup) nutritional yeast
1 vegetable stock cube
100 g baby spinach leaves

To serve
micro herbs (optional)
freshly ground black pepper
lemon wedges

Bring a large saucepan of water to the boil over high heat. Add the cauliflower and boil for 15 minutes or until soft and cooked through. Add the cashews about 1 minute before the cauliflower is ready, then drain and set aside.

Meanwhile, place a second large saucepan of water over high heat, add the salt and bring to the boil. Add the pasta and cook according to the packet instructions. Add the peas about 1 minute before the pasta is ready, then drain and transfer to a large bowl.

Heat 1 tablespoon of the olive oil in a frying pan over medium–high heat. Add the broccoli and sauté for 5 minutes or until golden and crisp. Remove the pan from the heat and set aside.

In a blender, combine the remaining olive oil, the soy milk, nutritional yeast and vegetable stock cube. Add the spinach, drained cauliflower and cashews and blend until smooth and bright green. Pour the green sauce over the pasta and peas and toss to combine.

Divide the pasta among bowls and top with the pan-fried broccoli. Scatter a few micro herbs over the top (if using), sprinkle with a little black pepper and serve with lemon wedges for squeezing over.

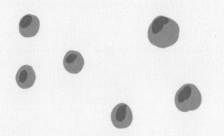

Baby/toddler friendly (omit the chilli and replace the wine with water)

Mushroom & leek
risotto

I've been making this risotto regularly for the past year and I absolutely adore it. The delicious flavour of the thyme and mushrooms, combined with the texture of the arborio rice makes for a very hearty and wholesome dinner (and leftover lunch).

Serves 4 / gf

1 litre (4 cups) vegetable stock
1 tablespoon olive oil
1 onion, finely diced
1 leek, white part only, finely sliced
2 garlic cloves, crushed
200 g brown mushrooms, sliced
330 g (1½ cups) arborio rice
125 ml (½ cup) vegan white wine
1 tablespoon thyme leaves
finely grated zest of 1 lemon
juice of ½ lemon

To serve
freshly ground black pepper
dried chilli flakes
vegan parmesan (for a recipe, see page 216)

Place the stock plus 250 ml (1 cup) of water in a large saucepan and bring to the boil, then remove from the heat, cover and set aside.

Heat the olive oil in another large saucepan over medium heat, add the onion, leek, garlic and mushroom and sauté for 3 minutes or until the onion is translucent. Add the rice and white wine and cook, stirring, until the wine is absorbed. Add the thyme leaves and 250 ml (1 cup) of the stock, then cover and cook, stirring occasionally, until the liquid is absorbed. Continue to add the stock, stirring and waiting until the liquid is absorbed before adding the next cup, until the rice is al dente. This should take about 15 minutes all up.

Remove from the heat and stir through the lemon zest and juice. Divide the risotto among bowls and serve topped with a little black pepper, a few chilli flakes and some vegan parmesan.

Honey & tamari
noodles

We can't get enough of noodles in our household, and I've recently discovered how delicious and quick it is to cook a healthy family dinner with instant noodles! This recipe makes great use of them, as well as fresh vegetables and a simple sauce. Feel free to replace the carrot and broccoli with any seasonal veggies that you and your family enjoy.

Serves 2 / gfo (use gf noodles and vegan chick'n tenders)

1 tablespoon olive oil
250 g vegan chick'n tenders (see Tip)
2 packets of dried instant noodles (you can also use soba or vermicelli rice noodles)
1 carrot, grated or julienned
1 small head of broccoli, cut into tiny florets
155 g (1 cup) frozen pea and corn mix
2 tablespoons tamari
2 tablespoons honey (or coconut nectar for a vegan option)

To serve (optional)
sriracha chilli sauce
1 teaspoon sesame seeds
1 spring onion, finely sliced
1 long red chilli, julienned

Place a large frying pan or wok over medium–high heat and add the oil. Once hot, add the vegan chick'n and fry for 3 minutes, stirring occasionally, or until golden.

Meanwhile, fill a large saucepan with water and bring to the boil. Add the noodles and cook according to the packet instructions.

While the noodles are cooking, add the veggies to the frying pan with the vegan chick'n and fry, stirring occasionally, for 3 minutes. Once the noodles are cooked, drain them and add to the pan along with the tamari, honey and 2 tablespoons of water. Toss the noodles and sauce through the veggies and cook for a further minute.

Remove the pan from the heat, divide the noodles among bowls and serve with whichever of the optional toppings you like.

Tip

I like The Meet Co's vegan chick'n tenders, but you can use firm tofu sliced into 2 cm strips instead if you prefer.

Fried rice
with chilli–coconut crunch

A good fried rice really hits the spot, and this one is no exception. I wanted to create a fried rice recipe that was quick and easy to make, while being packed with veggies and protein. The dry-fried coconut and fresh chilli on top add extra flavour and crunch, which I absolutely love.

Serves 4 / gf

400 g (2 cups) jasmine rice
1 tablespoon olive oil
300 g firm tofu, cut into 1 cm cubes
½ teaspoon Chinese five spice
2 spring onions, white and green parts
   separated, finely sliced
310 g (2 cups) frozen mixed veg (peas,
   corn and carrots)
sea salt and freshly ground black pepper
lime wedges, to serve

Chilli–coconut crunch
1 long red chilli (deseeded for less spice
   or omit for toddlers), finely sliced
30 g (½ cup) shredded coconut

Rinse the rice under cold running water, massaging it with your hands. Transfer to a rice cooker or saucepan and cook according to the packet instructions. Drain and set aside.

Meanwhile, to make the chilli–coconut crunch, heat a small frying pan over medium heat. Add the chilli and fry for 1 minute, then add the coconut and cook, stirring constantly, for 3 minutes or until the coconut is golden. Remove from the heat and set aside.

Heat the olive oil in a large frying pan over medium–high heat. Add the tofu and Chinese five spice and sauté for 4 minutes or until the tofu is golden all over. Add the white part of the spring onion and the frozen mixed veg and sauté for 2 minutes. Add the cooked rice and stir through the vegetable mixture for 2–3 minutes. Season with salt and pepper, to taste.

Divide the fried rice among bowls, top with the chilli–coconut crunch and green spring onion, and serve with lime wedges.

Baby/toddler friendly (replace the wine with water)

Simple tomato sauce
for pasta

The star of the show in this recipe is the oat cream, adding a smooth and delicious element to an already incredible tomato pasta sauce. Serve with plant-based ravioli or fresh linguine for a restaurant-style dinner in the comfort of your own home.

Serves 4–6 / gfo (use gf pasta)

1 tablespoon olive oil
80 g (½ cup) finely chopped red onion
3 garlic cloves, crushed
1 heaped tablespoon oregano leaves, finely chopped
2 × 400 g cans chopped tomatoes
½ teaspoon sea salt
¼ teaspoon freshly ground black pepper
125 ml (½ cup) oat cream, plus extra to serve
125 ml (½ cup) vegan white wine
500 g store-bought ravioli or pasta of your choice
50 g (½ cup) vegan parmesan (for a recipe, see page 216)
chopped mixed herbs, to serve (optional)

Heat the olive oil in a saucepan over high heat. Add the onion and sauté for 1½ minutes, until starting to soften, then add the garlic and oregano and sauté for 30 seconds. Add the tomatoes and salt and pepper, then reduce the heat to low, stir through the oat cream and white wine and simmer for 15 minutes, until slightly reduced.

While the tomato sauce is simmering, cook your pasta of choice according to the packet instructions. Drain.

Add the parmesan to the tomato sauce and simmer for a further 3 minutes, then remove from the heat and ladle the sauce into bowls. Add the cooked pasta, top with some chopped mixed herbs and a drizzle of extra oat cream, if you like, and serve.

Creamy ramen
with sweetcorn & tofu

Ramen is one of my favourite noodle dishes to make at home, and this recipe combines so many incredible flavours in one wholesome bowl. Traditional ramen can take days to make, but this vegan version is quick and simple to put together. It's also child friendly. A win–win–win!

Serves 2–4 / gfo (see Tip)

1 tablespoon olive oil
100 g (1 cup) finely sliced shiitake
   mushrooms
400 g canned sweetcorn kernels, rinsed
   and drained
2 spring onions, white and green parts
   separated, finely sliced
1 bunch of pak choy, white and green parts
   separated, finely sliced
200 g ramen noodles (or noodles of your
   choice, see Tip)
1 vegetable stock cube
375 ml (1½ cups) boiling water
1½ tablespoons white miso paste
1 tablespoon soy sauce or tamari
625 ml (2½ cups) oat milk (see Tip)
1 tablespoon sesame oil
300 g soft tofu, drained and cut into
   1–2 cm cubes
1 nori sheet, finely sliced
black and white sesame seeds, for sprinkling

To serve (optional)
sriracha chilli sauce
shichimi togarashi (see Tip, page 150)
chargrilled sweetcorn cobettes
chargrilled whole shiitake mushrooms

Heat the olive oil in a large saucepan over medium–high heat. Add the mushroom and sauté for 2 minutes, then add the corn kernels, white part of the spring onion and white part of the pak choy and sauté for another 2 minutes.

Meanwhile, bring a large saucepan of water to the boil over high heat, add the noodles and cook according to the packet instructions. Drain and set aside.

Crumble the vegetable stock cube into a bowl, add the boiling water and miso paste and stir to dissolve. Pour the mixture into the pan with the vegetables and add the soy sauce or tamari and oat milk. Bring to the boil, then remove the pan from the heat. Stir through the sesame oil and the green part of the pak choy.

Divide the noodles and tofu among serving bowls, then ladle the veggies and broth into the bowls, covering the noodles and tofu. Top with the green part of the spring onion, the shredded nori and a sprinkling of sesame seeds. If you like spice, add some sriracha chilli sauce and shichimi togarashi. For even more flavour, top with a couple of chargrilled sweetcorn cobettes and whole shiitake mushrooms. Serve straight away.

Tip

To make this recipe
gluten free, use rice
noodles instead of ramen
noodles, tamari instead
of soy sauce and sub in
gluten-free milk — cashew,
almond and soy all
work well.

Hearty baked
vegan meatballs

**These vegan meatballs pair perfectly with my simple tomato pasta sauce.
Really filling, easy to make and absolutely delicious, they are a great family dinner option
that can be kept and enjoyed for lunch the next day.**

Serves 4

2 tablespoons olive oil
½ onion, roughly chopped
3 small garlic cloves
165 g Swiss brown mushrooms, roughly chopped
400 g store-bought plant-based mince
  (see Tip)
2 teaspoons vegan Worcestershire sauce
2 teaspoons dried Italian herbs
½ teaspoon sea salt
freshly ground black pepper, to taste
1 large carrot, grated
150 g (1 cup) plain flour
Simple Tomato Sauce for Pasta (see page 167)
3 tablespoons vegan parmesan (for a recipe,
  see page 216)
1 tablespoon nutritional yeast (optional)
cooked spaghetti, to serve
oregano leaves, to serve

Preheat the oven to 180°C fan-forced. Grease a large baking dish with 1 tablespoon of the olive oil.

Place the onion, garlic and mushroom in a food processor and pulse for 30 seconds or until roughly chopped. Add the remaining olive oil, the plant-based mince, Worcestershire sauce, Italian herbs, salt and pepper and pulse for a further 10–15 seconds, just enough to bring together.

Transfer the meatball mixture to a large bowl and add the grated carrot. Sift in the flour and mix until well combined.

Use your hands to roll the meatball mixture into 5 cm balls. Place the balls 2.5 cm apart in the prepared baking dish.

Transfer the meatballs to the oven and bake for 20 minutes or until lightly golden. Remove from the oven, then pour over the simple tomato sauce and top with the vegan parmesan and nutritional yeast, if desired. Return to the oven for a further 5 minutes until the sauce is heated through.

Divide the spaghetti, meatballs and sauce among plates and serve warm with some oregano leaves sprinkled over the top.

Tip

I like to use
V2 plant-based mince
in these meatballs.

Toddler friendly (omit the chilli)

Cheesy rice
& black bean bake

This recipe uses microwavable rice to ensure a quick cooking time, making it the perfect midweek meal after a busy day at work. It's also packed full of veggies, with an umami kick from the vegan cheese. Keep it simple and serve the bake on its own or add some or all of the below serving suggestions, and enjoy for lunch or dinner with the whole family.

Serves 4 / gf

210 g (1 cup) microwavable brown rice
1 tablespoon olive oil
½ red onion, finely chopped
1 celery stalk, diced
1 red capsicum, diced
1 small zucchini, diced (or 1 sweetcorn cob, kernels stripped)
2 teaspoons smoked paprika
1 teaspoon ground cumin
¼ teaspoon cayenne pepper
2 teaspoons vegetable stock powder
250 g cherry tomatoes
400 g can black beans, rinsed and drained
2 teaspoons coconut sugar
40 g (⅓ cup) chopped walnuts
¼ teaspoon sea salt
pinch of freshly ground black pepper
½ cup grated vegan cheese, such as cheddar or gouda

To serve (optional)
corn chips
leafy salad
mashed avocado
sliced fresh jalapeño
chopped coriander leaves
coconut yoghurt
lime wedges

Preheat the oven to 200°C fan-forced.

Cook the rice in the microwave according to the packet instructions, then place in a large bowl and set aside.

Heat the olive oil in a large frying pan over medium heat, add the onion, celery, capsicum, zucchini, paprika, cumin, cayenne pepper and vegetable stock powder and cook for 8 minutes or until the vegetables are soft. Add the cherry tomatoes, black beans, coconut sugar, walnuts, salt and pepper. Add the brown rice and cook, stirring, for 1–2 minutes.

Transfer the rice mixture to a large baking dish and scatter the grated vegan cheese over the top. Bake for 8–10 minutes, until the cheese is melted and golden.

Serve the bake warm on its own or with your choice of corn chips, leafy salad, avocado, jalapeño, coriander, coconut yoghurt and lime wedges.

Slow Cooker Recipes

Massaman peanut stew

If you haven't tried mushroom meat before, this recipe is the perfect place to start. This massaman peanut stew is so hearty, and an easy slow cooker recipe for those days when you just don't have time to spend in the kitchen.

Serves 4 / gf

1 tablespoon olive oil
1 × quantity Massaman Curry Paste
  (see page 221)
1 red onion, cut into eighths
250 g Fable plant-based braised beef
  (see Tip) or 250 g shiitake mushrooms,
  roughly chopped
800 g potatoes, cut into 3 cm pieces
400 ml can coconut cream
2 tablespoons peanut butter
1 tablespoon coconut sugar
155 g (1 cup) frozen peas
To serve
steamed rice
sliced cucumber
sliced red chilli
roasted peanuts
fried shallots
lime wedges

Turn your slow cooker to the sauté setting. Add the olive oil and, once it is hot, add the curry paste and sauté for 1 minute. Add the onion and plant-based braised beef or shiitake mushroom and sauté for a further minute. Add the potato, coconut cream, 400 ml of water, the peanut butter and coconut sugar, then stir well and cover with the lid. Switch the slow cooker to low and cook for 6–8 hours, until the stew is reduced and thick.

With 5 minutes left on the slow cooker, add the peas, stir through and cover with the lid again.

Serve the massaman peanut stew with steamed rice, sliced cucumber and chilli, roasted peanuts, fried shallots and lime wedges for squeezing over.

Tip

You can purchase Fable plant-based braised beef at most supermarkets and vegan grocery stores.

Slow-cooked
eggplant ragu

Slow-cooked pasta sauce is a go-to in our household and this ragu
is a favourite. I love preparing it before a big day at work and coming home
to enjoy it for dinner, knowing all of the hard work has already been done.

Serves 4 / gfo (use gf pasta)

1 tablespoon olive oil or avocado oil
2 × 400 g cans chopped tomatoes
400 g can lentils, rinsed and drained
1 eggplant, finely diced
1 onion, finely diced
2 garlic cloves, crushed
250 g cherry tomatoes
2 teaspoons vegetable stock powder
freshly ground black pepper, to taste
2 teaspoons dried Italian herbs
1 tablespoon olive tapenade
80 ml (⅓ cup) vegan red wine
1 tablespoon balsamic vinegar

To serve
your choice of pasta
chopped oregano or flat-leaf parsley leaves
  (optional)

This recipe is so easy! Add all of the ingredients
to your slow cooker, then cover with the lid and
cook on low for 6–8 hours or high for 3–4 hours, until
reduced and thick.

When the ragu is almost ready, bring a large
saucepan of salted water to the boil and cook the
pasta according to the packet instructions until al
dente. Drain.

Divide the pasta among serving bowls, top with the
slow-cooked eggplant ragu and scatter over some
oregano or parsley, if you like. Enjoy!

Butter cauliflower curry

I recently invested in a slow cooker and, not to be too dramatic, but it's been life changing.
The slow cooker makes preparing dishes like this nourishing cauliflower curry so easy.
I hope this dish becomes a staple in your household, as it is in mine.

Serves 4 / gf

1 tablespoon avocado oil
1 head of cauliflower, chopped into florets
400 g can chopped tomatoes
1 tablespoon coconut sugar
1 vegetable stock cube
250 g (1 cup) natural coconut yoghurt
155 g (1 cup) frozen peas
juice of ½ lemon

Curry paste
1 teaspoon ground turmeric
2 teaspoons garam masala
2 teaspoons ground cumin
2.5 cm piece of ginger, grated
2 garlic cloves, crushed
1 long red chilli, roughly chopped

To serve
steamed rice
finely chopped coriander leaves
natural coconut yoghurt
freshly ground black pepper
finely chopped red chilli

To make the curry paste, place all of the ingredients in a blender and blend to a smooth paste.

Turn your slow cooker to the sauté setting. Add the avocado oil and, once it is hot, add the curry paste and sauté for 1 minute. Add the cauliflower florets, tossing through and sautéing for a further minute. Add the tomatoes, coconut sugar, vegetable stock cube and coconut yoghurt. Stir well, then cover with the lid, switch the slow cooker to low and cook for 7–8 hours, until the cauliflower falls apart when tested with a fork and the sauce is nicely reduced.

Before serving, add the peas to the slow cooker and stir through. Cover with the lid and cook for 5–10 minutes, until the peas are soft. Add the lemon juice right before serving.

Serve the butter cauliflower curry with steamed rice, coriander leaves, coconut yoghurt, a little black pepper and red chilli.

Toddler friendly

Classic
winter minestrone

Minestrone is such a wonderfully hearty and warming dinner, and using a slow cooker makes it even easier to prepare! Filled with lots of nutritious vegetables, I love serving this soup with thick-cut bread on a cold winter's night.

Serves 4 / gfo (use gf pasta and bread)

1 tablespoon olive oil
2 celery stalks, sliced
1 leek, white part only, halved lengthways and sliced
1 carrot, quartered and sliced
1 French shallot, finely chopped
3 garlic cloves, crushed
280 g potatoes, cut into 1 cm pieces
3 bay leaves
2 teaspoons dried Italian herbs
400 g can cannellini beans, rinsed and drained
1.5 litres vegetable stock
2 × 400 g cans crushed tomatoes
¼ teaspoon sea salt
freshly ground black pepper, to taste, plus extra to serve
100 g pasta shells
thick-cut bread, to serve (optional)

Turn your slow cooker to the sauté setting. Add the olive oil and, once it is hot, add the celery, leek, carrot, shallot and garlic and sauté for 2–3 minutes, until the vegetables have softened.

Switch the slow cooker to high, add the remaining ingredients except the pasta and mix lightly, then cover with the lid and cook for 3 hours.

Add the pasta shells to the slow cooker and stir them through. Cover with the lid and continue to cook on high for another hour or until the pasta shells are cooked through.

Serve hot, with a good sprinkling of freshly ground black pepper and some thick-cut bread on the side, if desired.

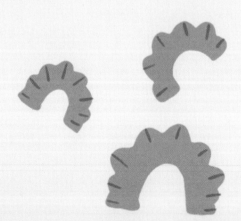

Dad's curried
vegan sausages

Whenever I think of curried sausages, I think of my dad. This is one of his favourite dishes and I really enjoyed recreating it for this cookbook! Using a slow cooker for simplicity, this dish is packed with flavour, heartiness and loads of veggies.

Serves 4

1 tablespoon olive oil
6 plant-based sausages (see Tip), cut into quarters
1 onion, halved and cut into wedges
1 red capsicum, cut into 2 cm pieces
1 carrot, halved lengthways and sliced
2 small potatoes (about 260 g), cut into 2.5 cm pieces
¾ teaspoon sea salt
freshly ground black pepper, to taste
2 tablespoons curry powder
½ teaspoon ground turmeric
½ teaspoon dried chilli flakes
2 × 400 ml cans coconut cream
155 g (1 cup) frozen peas

To serve
steamed rice
coriander leaves
toasted coconut flakes (optional)

Tip
I like to use Vegie Delights brand sausages in this recipe.

Turn your slow cooker to the sauté setting. Add the olive oil and, once it is hot, add the sausages and fry for 3–5 minutes, until lightly golden.

Switch the slow cooker to high and add the onion, capsicum, carrot, potato, salt, pepper, curry powder, turmeric, chilli, coconut cream and 400 ml of water. Cover with the lid and cook for 4–6 hours.

Add the peas, cover and continue to cook for a further 30 minutes.

Serve the curried sausages with rice, topped with coriander leaves and coconut flakes, if desired.

Any leftover curried sausages will keep in an airtight container in the freezer for up to 1 month.

One-pot
veggie con carne

This is one of my go-to slow cooker recipes. Packed full of hearty vegetables, this one-pot meal always makes me feel amazing, plus it's high in protein with the addition of both TVP and black beans. Serve with corn chips, avocado and herbs for a fresh lunch or dinner.

Serves 4 / gf

1 tablespoon olive oil
1 onion, finely diced
2 large garlic cloves, crushed
3 celery stalks, finely diced
2 small carrots, finely diced
¼ teaspoon cayenne pepper
2 teaspoons smoked paprika
2 teaspoons ground cumin
2 × 400 g cans chopped tomatoes
2 × 400 g cans black beans, rinsed and drained
220 g (2 cups) TVP (Textured Vegetable Protein)
2 vegetable stock cubes
1 teaspoon sea salt
freshly ground black pepper, to taste

To serve (optional)
corn chips
diced avocado
chopped coriander leaves
natural coconut yoghurt
sliced red chilli

Turn your slow cooker to the sauté setting. Add the olive oil and, once it is hot, add the onion, garlic, celery, carrot, cayenne pepper, paprika and cumin and sauté for 2–3 minutes, until the onion has softened.

Add the tomatoes, black beans and TVP to the slow cooker and give everything a really good stir. Add 800 ml of water and crumble in the vegetable stock cubes. Season with the salt and pepper and mix well. Switch the slow cooker to high, cover with the lid and cook for 4 hours.

Once ready, serve the veggie con carne with your choice of corn chips, diced avocado, coriander leaves, coconut yoghurt and sliced red chilli.

Creamy pumpkin & tofu curry

Pumpkin is such a hearty and versatile winter vegetable, and it goes perfectly in this slow-cooked curry. Prepare this in the morning and enjoy as a nourishing weeknight dinner.

Serves 4 / gf

1 tablespoon olive oil
114 g can Maesri Panang curry paste (or to make your own Red Laksa Curry Paste, see page 222)
600 g pumpkin (any variety is fine), skin on, cut into 2 cm cubes
½ onion, cut into large chunks
300 g firm tofu, cut into 2 cm cubes
400 ml can coconut cream
2 teaspoons vegetable stock powder
1 tablespoon finely chopped coriander root
100 g baby spinach leaves
juice of 1 lime
sea salt and freshly ground black pepper

To serve
steamed rice
finely grated lime zest
chopped coriander leaves
sliced cucumber (optional)
sliced red chilli (optional)
chopped dill fronds (optional)
lime wedges

Turn your slow cooker to the sauté setting. Add the olive oil and, once it is hot, add the curry paste and sauté for 1 minute or until fragrant. Add the pumpkin and onion and stir well to coat in the curry paste. Add the tofu and sauté for 1 minute, then add the coconut cream, 250 ml (1 cup) of water, the vegetable stock powder and coriander root and stir to combine. Switch the slow cooker to low, cover with the lid and cook for 7–8 hours, until the pumpkin is cooked through and the curry sauce has thickened.

Add the spinach, then cover and cook for a final 10 minutes. Switch off the heat, stir through the lime juice and season with salt and pepper to taste.

Divide some steamed rice among bowls and spoon over the curry. Sprinkle a little lime zest and a few chopped coriander leaves over the curry and serve with sliced cucumber, sliced red chilli and chopped dill fronds, if desired, and lime wedges for squeezing over.

Homemade coconut yoghurt

Cheat's sour cream

Speedy cashew pesto

Cheesy queso sauce

Tahini ranch dressing

Zesty salsa verde

Guacamole with jalapeño

Vegan feta & parmesan

Massaman curry paste

Red laksa curry paste

Pickled red onion

Condiments & Staples

Baby/toddler friendly

Homemade
coconut yoghurt

We eat so much coconut yoghurt in my household, so I thought it was about time we made it ourselves! This is such a fun staple to make and while it takes time – you'll need to start this a day ahead – it is very simple and rewarding to create.

Makes about 400 g / gf

400 ml can coconut milk
4 g probiotic powder (about 30 billion CFU, no prebiotics)
1 tablespoon cornflour

Place the coconut milk and probiotic powder in a large sterilised jar (see Tips). Sift in the cornflour and mix well with a sterilised wooden spoon.

Cover the jar with a piece of muslin cloth and an elastic band and leave to sit overnight in a warm spot (away from direct sunlight, but do not refrigerate).

The next day, transfer the jar to the fridge and enjoy for up to 1 week. Use the yoghurt to make smoothie popsicles (see page 244) and cheat's sour cream (see page 201), and serve with desserts such as my 5-minute chocolate puddings (see page 258) and ginger–caramel pudding (see page 264).

Tips

To sterilise the jar and wooden spoon, bring a large saucepan of water to the boil. Add the jar, lid and spoon and boil, submerged, for 5 minutes. Using clean tongs, lift out the jar, lid and spoon and leave to air-dry on a clean tea towel until completely dry.

Don't have a muslin cloth? This is a great time to repurpose an old baby swaddle!

Cheat's
sour cream

This is an easy and delicious alternative to sour cream that is super quick to make. It's also really versatile – use it as a topping for nachos, on tacos or as a fantastic dipping sauce.

Makes 250 g (1 cup) / gf

250 g (1 cup) natural coconut yoghurt
  (for a recipe, see page 198)
1 tablespoon freshly squeezed lemon juice

Place the coconut yoghurt and lemon juice in a small bowl and stir to combine.

Serve the sour cream on top of nachos, tacos or other Mexican dishes. It also make a great dipping sauce – try it with my crispy lemon pepper cauliflower on page 130.

Store the sour cream in an airtight container or jar in the fridge for up to 3 days.

Tip

Lightly stir some sweet chilli sauce or sriracha chilli sauce through the sour cream for a sweet or spicy kick!

Speedy
cashew pesto

I love making pesto at home as it is so easy and packed full of flavour. Vegan parmesan is increasingly available in supermarkets these days and it works really well in this recipe. This pesto is the perfect addition to pasta salad (see page 118) and also tastes amazing added to toasted sandwiches (see page 65).

Makes 200 g / gf

3 tablespoons olive oil
½ teaspoon sea salt
3 tablespoons freshly squeezed lemon juice
3 tablespoons vegan parmesan (for a recipe, see page 216)
45 g (1 cup firmly packed) baby spinach leaves
50 g (1 cup firmly packed) basil leaves
80 g (½ cup) raw cashews

Place the olive oil, salt, lemon juice, vegan parmesan and spinach in a high-speed blender and blend until smooth. Add the basil leaves and cashews and pulse for 30 seconds.

Store the pesto in an airtight container or jar in the fridge for up to 3 days.

Cheesy queso
sauce

I am absolutely obsessed with this queso sauce! It pairs perfectly with roasted veggies and is great on nachos or as a delicious dip. The recipe calls for nacho seasoning, which is a super simple ingredient that adds a big punch of flavour. Try serving this sauce with my crispy potatoes on page 124.

Makes 750 ml (3 cups) / gf

1 carrot, chopped
1 large potato, peeled and chopped
155 g (1 cup) raw cashews
30 g sachet of nacho seasoning
15 g (¼ cup) nutritional yeast
125 ml (½ cup) soy milk
2 tablespoons freshly squeezed lemon juice
sea salt

To serve (optional)
chopped coriander leaves
smoked paprika

Bring a large saucepan of water to the boil over high heat, then add the carrot and potato. Reduce the heat to a simmer, then cover and cook for 15 minutes or until the carrot is soft and the potato is easily pierced with a knife. Add the cashews and simmer for 1 minute, then drain and transfer to a blender.

Add the nacho seasoning, nutritional yeast, soy milk and lemon juice to the blender and blend until smooth. Taste and season with salt, if needed, then transfer to a serving bowl and top with some chopped coriander and smoked paprika, if desired.

Store the queso sauce in an airtight container or jar in the fridge for up to 3 days.

Tahini
ranch dressing

This super-quick ranch dressing is very easy to make and the perfect accompaniment to roasted veggies and my air-fried lemon pepper cauliflower (see page 130).

Makes about 340 ml / gf

205 g (¾ cup) hulled tahini
1½ tablespoons maple syrup
½ teaspoon sea salt
1 tablespoon chopped dill fronds,
  plus extra to serve (optional)

Place the tahini, maple syrup, 125 ml (½ cup) of water, the salt and dill fronds in a small bowl and whisk until smooth. If the dressing is too thick, add another tablespoon or so of water to thin it out a little.

Transfer the dressing to a small bowl, top with some extra dill, if you like, and serve with your favourite salad or roasted veggies.

Store the tahini ranch dressing in an airtight container or jar in the fridge for up to 3 days.

Zesty
salsa verde

This salsa verde is fresh and packed full of flavour. The red onion adds a delightful crunch while the lemon juice provides a lovely zing that brightens up the sauce. Try it with my smoky cauliflower steaks on page 148 or as a dressing for roasted veggies.

Serves 4 / gf

small handful of flat-leaf parsley leaves
1 tablespoon finely chopped red onion
2 garlic cloves, crushed
2 tablespoons freshly squeezed lemon juice
2 tablespoons olive oil
½ teaspoon sea salt

Place the parsley, red onion and garlic in a blender or the small bowl of a food processor and pulse until chopped but still a little chunky.

Transfer to a small bowl, then add the lemon juice, olive oil and salt and mix well. Serve immediately.

Store the salsa verde in an airtight container or jar in the fridge for up to 3 days.

Guacamole
with jalapeño

Guacamole is such a staple in our household. Whether it's on top of nachos, with tacos or even as a snack, I love using this classic condiment to bring flavour to a wide range of dishes. With only five ingredients, it's very simple and can be prepared in just minutes!

Makes 2 cups / gf

- 2 avocados
- ½ teaspoon sea salt flakes
- 1 tablespoon freshly squeezed lime juice (from about ½ lime), plus lime wedges to serve
- 1 tablespoon roughly chopped coriander leaves, plus extra to serve
- ¼ fresh jalapeño, deseeded and finely diced

Mash the avocado, salt, lime juice, coriander and jalapeño in a small bowl.

Transfer to a serving bowl and top with extra coriander leaves and lime wedges, if you like. This guacamole is best eaten straight away – serve it with corn chips for dipping or on top of nachos with my cheat's sour cream (see page 201).

Tip

If you like your guacamole spicy, add an extra quarter of sliced fresh jalapeño for a real kick!

Vegan
feta & parmesan

Vegan feta and parmesan are readily available from health food stores and
even some supermarkets these days but it's fun to make your own if you have the time.
This feta recipe uses a mix of almonds and cashews, and is super creamy and delicious.
Vegan parmesan is the perfect addition to salads, pasta dishes and so much more!

Vegan feta

Makes 1 × 500 ml jar / gf

155 g (1 cup) blanched almonds, soaked in
  cold water overnight
35 g cashews, soaked in cold water overnight
3 tablespoons olive oil, plus extra to cover
3 tablespoons freshly squeezed lemon juice
½ teaspoon sea salt
1 tablespoon nutritional yeast
3 rosemary sprigs
1 teaspoon black peppercorns
peeled zest of 1 lemon

Line a 20 cm × 10 cm loaf tin with baking paper.

Drain and rinse the nuts, then transfer to a
high-speed blender and add the olive oil, lemon
juice, salt, nutritional yeast and 3 tablespoons of
water. Blend on high speed for about 10 minutes,
stopping occasionally to scrape down the side,
until thick and completely smooth.

Transfer to the tin and press down using a spatula.
Cover and refrigerate for 1–2 hours, until set.

Remove the feta from the tin and cut into 1.5 cm
thick slices. Place in a clean 500 ml jar and add
the rosemary, peppercorns and lemon zest. Fill the
jar with extra olive oil, then seal and place in the
fridge. The feta will keep for up to 1 week.

Vegan parmesan

Makes 130 g (1¼ cups) / gf

155 g (1 cup) cashews
30 g (½ cup) nutritional yeast
½ teaspoon garlic powder
½ teaspoon sea salt
¼ teaspoon freshly ground black pepper
  (optional)

Place all of the ingredients in a high-speed blender
and blend until a fine crumb is formed.

Store in an airtight container or jar in the fridge for
up to 1 week.

Tip

I love making this
vegan parmesan and keeping it
in the fridge to enjoy on top
of some of my favourite dishes.
It is delicious on my hearty
baked meatballs (see page 173)
mushroom and leek risotto
(see page 160) and
spicy corn ribs
(see page 92).

Massaman
curry paste

This massaman curry paste recipe is based on the massaman curry recipe in my second book, *The Global Vegan*. It is surprisingly quick to make, incredibly fragrant and the perfect base for my massaman peanut stew (see page 178).

Serves 4 / gf

5 long red chillies, chopped
½ teaspoon black peppercorns
2 teaspoons ground coriander
½ teaspoon cumin seeds
¼ teaspoon ground allspice
1 teaspoon sea salt
½ teaspoon ground cinnamon
2 garlic cloves
1 red Asian shallot, roughly chopped
2 cardamom pods
1 teaspoon ground turmeric
2 teaspoons chopped coriander root
1 tablespoon avocado oil

Place all of the ingredients in a high-speed blender and blend for 1 minute or until smooth.

Transfer to an airtight container or jar and store in the fridge for up to 5 days or the freezer for up to 1 month.

Red laksa
curry paste

This red laksa paste is flavoured with fragrant lemongrass and ginger, and it is one of my favourites to cook with. Use it as the base for my creamy pumpkin and tofu curry (see page 195).

Serves 4 / gf

1 lemongrass stalk, white part only
3 garlic cloves
4 cm piece of ginger, peeled and chopped
2 long red chillies
2 tablespoons chopped coriander root
½ teaspoon ground coriander
¼ teaspoon ground cumin
½ teaspoon ground turmeric
¼ teaspoon freshly ground black pepper
1 teaspoon sea salt
1 tablespoon coconut sugar
1 tablespoon avocado oil

Place all of the ingredients in a high-speed blender and blend for 1 minute or until smooth.

Transfer to an airtight container or jar and store in the fridge for up to 5 days or the freezer for up to 1 month.

Tip

Make a double batch of this curry paste and use it in the Singaporean laksa from my second cookbook, *The Global Vegan*.

Condiments & Staples

Pickled
red onion

I absolutely love having this pickled red onion in the fridge to serve on top of a variety of my favourite savoury dishes. It's super simple to make and adds an extra hit of flavour and welcome crunch to your meal.

Makes 500 ml / gf

1 red onion, finely sliced
2 teaspoons sea salt
300 ml lukewarm water
1 tablespoon apple cider vinegar
1 tablespoon maple syrup
1 fresh jalapeño, finely sliced (optional, but great if you love spice and for serving with Mexican food!)

Place all of the ingredients in a large mason jar. Screw the lid on and shake well to combine.

Transfer to the fridge for a minimum of 3 hours to allow the flavours to develop. The pickled red onion will keep in the fridge for up to 1 week.

Tip

Try serving this pickled onion with tacos, my cheesy rice and black bean bake (see page 174) or with fresh guacamole (see page 214) and corn chips.

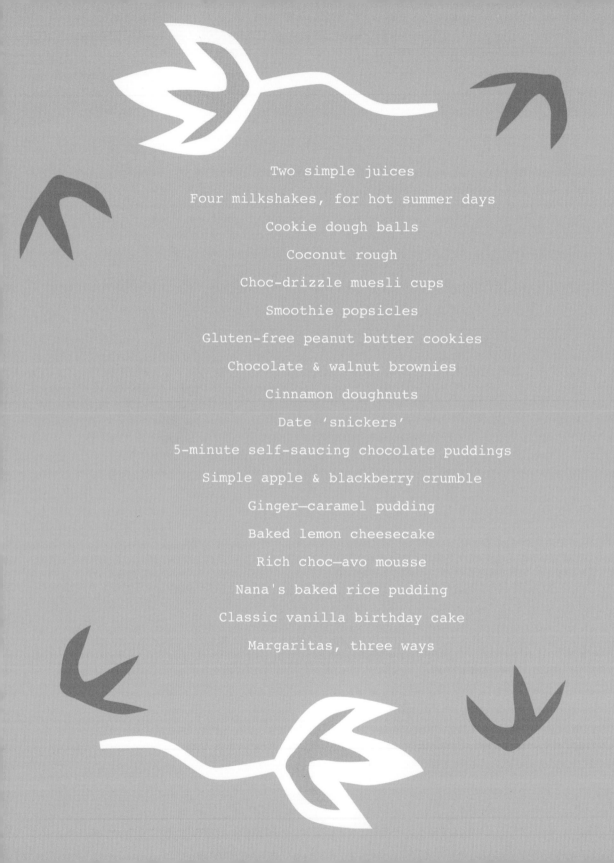

Two simple juices

Four milkshakes, for hot summer days

Cookie dough balls

Coconut rough

Choc-drizzle muesli cups

Smoothie popsicles

Gluten-free peanut butter cookies

Chocolate & walnut brownies

Cinnamon doughnuts

Date 'snickers'

5-minute self-saucing chocolate puddings

Simple apple & blackberry crumble

Ginger—caramel pudding

Baked lemon cheesecake

Rich choc—avo mousse

Nana's baked rice pudding

Classic vanilla birthday cake

Margaritas, three ways

Sweets
& Drinks

Two simple
juices

Here are two of my favourite simple juice blends! I love a sour profile when it comes to juice,
so I've given you my top two sour juices in green and pink.

Sour greenie

Makes 1 litre / gf

4 celery stalks
1 long cucumber, cut into small pieces
4 green apples, each cut into 8 wedges
3 lemons, rind removed and cut into quarters

Strawberry lemonade

Makes 1 litre / gf

½ pineapple, skin removed and cut into
  5 cm pieces
3 lemons, rind removed and cut into quarters
250 g punnet of strawberries, hulled
400 ml ice-cold water

Add all of the ingredients to a juicer (see Tip), then juice and enjoy!

As both of these juices are very sour from the lemons, I top them up with water, just like a homemade lemonade. Add enough water to each juice to make 1 litre.

Both juices will keep in airtight bottles in the fridge for up to 3 days, but are best used within 1–2 days for more nutrition. Shake before pouring.

Tip

I recommend investing in a cold-press juicer. It produces a higher quality juice as no heat is used in the extraction process.

Four milkshakes,
for hot summer days

I love a good milkshake – even more so when there are four to choose from!
These milkshakes remind me of summer days at the beach with friends and family.

Chocolate

Serves 1 / gfo (use gf plant milk instead
of oat milk)

2 scoops (½ cup) vegan vanilla ice cream
250 ml (1 cup) oat milk
1 tablespoon cacao powder
1 teaspoon maple syrup
pinch of sea salt
vegan chocolate chips and chocolate sauce,
  to decorate (optional)

Vanilla–coconut

Serves 1 / gf

2 scoops (½ cup) vegan vanilla ice cream
250 ml (1 cup) coconut milk
1 tablespoon desiccated coconut, plus extra
  to decorate
1 teaspoon maple syrup, plus extra
  to drizzle
½ teaspoon vanilla extract

Sweets & Drinks

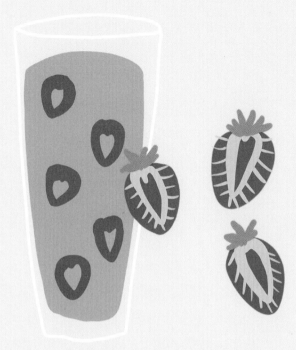

Strawberry

Serves 1 / gfo (use gf plant milk instead of oat milk)

2 scoops (½ cup) vegan vanilla ice cream
250 ml (1 cup) oat milk
6 strawberries, hulled
1 teaspoon maple syrup
¼ teaspoon vanilla extract
vegan sprinkles and strawberry sauce,
  to decorate (optional)

Espresso

Serves 1 / gfo (use gf plant milk instead of oat milk)

2 scoops (½ cup) vegan vanilla ice cream
250 ml (1 cup) oat milk
1 shot of espresso
1 teaspoon maple syrup, plus extra
  to drizzle

Choose a flavour combo (or make all four!) and add all of the ingredients to a high-speed blender. Blend until smooth, then pour into your favourite milkshake glass, decorate with any toppings that you like and enjoy!

Chocolate milkshake, see page 234

Vanilla-coconut milkshake, see page 234

Strawberry milkshake, see page 235

Espresso milkshake, see page 235

cookie dough
balls

You know when that 4 pm sweet craving hits some days? These cookie dough balls are the perfect snack to satisfy you. This is a great little recipe to get the kids involved with rolling the cookie dough into balls. Prepare them on the weekend and enjoy them throughout the week – this recipe makes enough to keep the whole family satisfied.

Makes 16–18 / gf

3 tablespoons almond butter
3 tablespoons solid coconut oil
150 g (1 cup) pitted medjool dates
1 teaspoon vanilla extract
240 g (2⅓ cups) almond meal
120 g (¾ cup) vegan chocolate chips

Place all of the ingredients except the chocolate chips in a food processor and process until well combined and sticky.

Transfer the mixture to a bowl, add the chocolate chips and mix through with your hands.

Scoop heaped tablespoons of dough and roll into 16–18 even-sized balls.

Store the cookie dough balls in an airtight container in the fridge, where they will keep for up to 1 week. Alternatively, you can store them in the freezer for up to 1 month.

Coconut
rough

This is a fun take on the timeless classic, except that my version is packed full of nutrients with the inclusion of buckinis and hemp seeds. I love preparing it in advance to enjoy as a sweet treat throughout the week!

Makes 6 / gf

170 g (1 cup) vegan dark chocolate chips
1½ tablespoons coconut oil
60 g (1 cup) shredded coconut
3 tablespoons buckinis (see Tip)
1 tablespoon hemp seeds
pinch of sea salt flakes

Line a baking tray with baking paper.

Place the chocolate chips and coconut oil in a microwave-safe bowl, then microwave on high for 1½ minutes or until melted. Gently stir to combine, then add the shredded coconut, buckinis and hemp seeds and stir through.

Using a dessert spoon, spoon six even-sized mounds onto the prepared tray and flatten into 8 cm discs. Place in the fridge for 1 hour to set before enjoying.

The coconut rough will keep in an airtight container in the fridge for up to 1 week.

Tip

Buckinis are buckwheat kernels that have been soaked and then dried. They are available from health food stores and some supermarkets.

Choc-drizzle
muesli cups

These muesli cups are the ultimate lunchbox snack! Nut free, sesame free and gluten free, they are perfect for kids and adults alike as an afternoon treat.

Makes 12 / gf

25 g (1 cup) puffed rice
25 g (1 cup) puffed quinoa
½ teaspoon sea salt flakes, plus extra
   to serve (optional)
80 ml (⅓ cup) maple syrup
50 g (⅓ cup) hemp seeds
80 ml (⅓ cup) coconut oil
1 tablespoon flaxseed meal
200 g (1 cup) buckinis (see Tip, page 241)
   or buckwheat groats
3 tablespoons vegan chocolate chips

Preheat the oven to 170°C fan-forced. Grease a 12-hole cupcake tin (silicone moulds work best for easy removal). Line a baking tray with baking paper.

Combine all of the ingredients except the chocolate chips in a large bowl. Divide the mixture between the holes of the cupcake tin, then bake for 20 minutes or until lightly golden.

Allow the muesli cups to cool in the muffin trays, then turn out onto the prepared baking tray.

Melt the chocolate chips in a microwave on high for 1 minute. Gently stir the melted chocolate, then, using a spoon, drizzle the chocolate over the muesli cups. Place in the fridge for 1 hour to set, then sprinkle with a little extra salt just before serving, if you like.

The muesli cups will keep in an airtight container in the fridge for up to 1 week.

Sweets & Drinks

Smoothie popsicles

I really enjoy making these simple smoothie popsicles for my son, Bowie,
and I love watching him devour them. They are an excellent sweet treat,
as they are packed full of healthy fats and fresh berries.

Makes 6 / gf

125 g (½ cup) vanilla coconut yoghurt
1 teaspoon flaxseed meal
100 g fresh berries of your choice, larger
  berries chopped (see Tip)

Place the coconut yoghurt, flaxseed meal and
berries in a bowl. Mix until well combined.

Distribute the mixture evenly among six 250 ml
(1 cup) popsicle moulds, then place in the freezer
to set for at least 4 hours or overnight.

Enjoy straight from the freezer!

Tip

I like to use a
mix of raspberries and
blackberries for these
popsicles, but you can
use any combination of
berries you like.

Gluten-free
peanut butter cookies

We love peanut butter in my household, and these cookies especially are a huge hit!
Top them with chocolate chips for a little extra decadence (although they're just
as good without), and serve with a cup of your favourite tea.

Makes 10 / gf

1 tablespoon flaxseed meal
1 tablespoon soy milk
125 ml (½ cup) vegan butter, cubed and
  softened
60 g (½ cup) coconut sugar
125 g (½ cup) peanut butter
1 teaspoon vanilla extract
¼ teaspoon sea salt flakes
250 g (1½ cups) plain gluten-free flour
  (see Tip, page 114)
½ teaspoon baking powder
handful of vegan chocolate chips (optional)

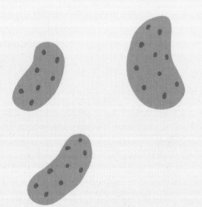

Preheat the oven to 170°C fan-forced. Line a baking tray with baking paper.

Combine the flaxseed meal and soy milk in a small bowl and set aside.

Place the vegan butter and coconut sugar in a large bowl and mix with electric beaters for about 1 minute, until pale and fluffy. Add the peanut butter, flaxseed mixture, vanilla extract and salt and beat until well combined. Sift the flour and baking powder into the bowl and stir through using a spatula.

Rolled heaped tablespoons of the dough into balls and place on the prepared tray. Top with some chocolate chips, if desired, then bake for 12 minutes or until lightly golden, with slightly cracked edges.

Allow the cookies to cool on the tray for 30 minutes, then transfer to a wire rack to cool completely.

The cookies will keep in an airtight container for up to 1 week.

chocolate & walnut
brownies

Who doesn't love a good brownie? These ones, with the addition of walnuts, are my absolute favourite and you can easily make them gluten free by changing the flour (see Tip). They are subtly sweet, deliciously decadent and perfect served warm with vegan ice cream.

Makes 12–16 / gfo (see Tip)

3 tablespoons flaxseed meal
120 g (1 cup) coconut sugar
125 ml (½ cup) olive oil
2 teaspoons vanilla extract
250 ml (1 cup) soy milk
100 g (1 cup) cacao powder
150 g (1 cup) plain flour
½ teaspoon sea salt
90 g (¾ cup) crushed walnuts
vegan vanilla ice cream, to serve (optional)

Tip

To make these gluten free, simply replace the 150 g of plain flour with 130 g of gluten-free flour (I like to use Orgran brand) and 70 g of almond meal.

Place the flaxseed meal in a small bowl, add 125 ml (½ cup) of water, then whisk and set aside for 2 minutes.

Preheat the oven to 170°C fan-forced and line the base and sides of a 20 cm square baking tin with baking paper.

Add the flaxseed gel, coconut sugar, olive oil and vanilla extract to a blender and blend on high speed for 15 seconds. Add the soy milk and blend for a further 15 seconds. Transfer to a large bowl.

Sift the cacao powder, flour and salt over the wet ingredients, then fold through until just combined (small pockets of unmixed flour are okay). Add 60 g (½ cup) of the walnuts and fold them through.

Pour the mixture into the prepared tin and gently wobble the tin to distribute the batter evenly. Sprinkle with the remaining walnuts, then transfer to the oven and bake for 20–25 minutes, until lightly golden and slightly crisp on top.

Set the brownies aside to cool for 10 minutes, then transfer to a wire rack to cool for a further 10 minutes. Slice into 12–16 pieces and serve warm with some vegan ice cream, if you like.

The brownies will keep in an airtight container in the fridge for up to 5 days.

Cinnamon
doughnuts

I'm so obsessed with the cinnamon doughnuts at my local market that I decided to try creating my own at home. These doughnuts are baked, not fried, making them a healthier option. They are deliciously sweet and simple to make.

Makes 10

150 g (1 cup) self-raising flour
60 g (½ cup) coconut sugar
¼ teaspoon sea salt
½ teaspoon ground cinnamon
185 ml (¾ cup) soy milk
1 teaspoon vanilla extract
2 tablespoons melted vegan butter, plus extra for greasing

To coat

60 g (½ cup) coconut sugar
1 teaspoon ground cinnamon
2 tablespoons melted vegan butter

Preheat the oven to 180°C fan-forced. Grease ten doughnut moulds with vegan butter.

Sift the flour, coconut sugar, salt and cinnamon into a large bowl. Add the soy milk, vanilla extract and melted vegan butter and stir until just combined. Spoon the batter into the moulds, ensuring the moulds are only half full.

Place the moulds on a large baking tray and pop them in the oven to bake for 9–10 minutes, until risen and lightly golden on top. Allow the doughnuts to cool in the moulds for 10 minutes before turning out onto a wire rack.

While the doughnuts are cooling, combine the coconut sugar and cinnamon for coating in a shallow bowl. Brush the doughnuts with the melted vegan butter, then roll them in the sugar and cinnamon, ensuring they are generously coated. Serve straight away.

Sweets & Drinks

Date
'snickers'

This recipe has been a staple for me for years! It's a simple, healthy alternative to the famous caramel and peanut chocolate bar and is a great snack to make in advance and enjoy whenever you have a sweet craving.

Makes 16 / gf

16 medjool dates
2½ tablespoons smooth peanut butter
2 tablespoons crushed peanuts
200 g vegan dark chocolate, roughly chopped
2 tablespoons solid coconut oil
½ teaspoon sea salt flakes

Slice the dates lengthways down the centre and remove the pits, ensuring you don't slice all the way through. Fill the dates with the peanut butter and top with 1½ tablespoons of the crushed peanuts, pushing the nuts into the peanut butter.

Place the chocolate and coconut oil in a small microwave-safe bowl, then microwave on high for 1½ minutes or until melted. Stir the melted chocolate and coconut oil until smooth, then dip the dates into the mixture, ensuring they are fully coated. Transfer to a wire rack with paper towel underneath, for the excess chocolate to drip onto. Once all of the dates are coated, place them in the fridge to harden for 30 minutes.

Remove the dates from the fridge and dip them back in the chocolate mixture (you may need to briefly remelt the chocolate mixture in the microwave). Once coated, place the dates back on the wire rack and sprinkle with the remaining crushed peanuts and the salt. Return to the fridge for a further 15 minutes, then enjoy.

The date 'snickers' will keep in an airtight container in the fridge for up to 1 week.

5-minute
self-saucing chocolate puddings

The only thing better than self-saucing chocolate puddings are self-saucing chocolate puddings that are ready in 5 minutes! This is such a quick, low-effort and decadent dessert – I really hope you give it a try.

Serves 2

3 tablespoons self-raising flour
60 g (½ cup) coconut sugar
1¾ tablespoons cacao powder
3 tablespoons soy milk
½ teaspoon vanilla extract
2 tablespoons olive oil
pinch of sea salt
3 tablespoons boiling water
oat pouring cream or vegan vanilla
  ice cream, to serve

Sift the flour, three-quarters of the coconut sugar and all but 1 teaspoon of the cacao powder into a bowl. Add the soy milk, vanilla extract and olive oil and whisk together to form a batter.

Evenly divide the batter between two small, deep microwave-safe bowls. Sprinkle the salt and the remaining coconut sugar and cacao powder over the batter, then carefully pour over the boiling water.

Microwave on high for 1½ minutes, until the puddings are firm around the edge but still a bit gooey in the middle.

Serve the puddings with dollops of oat cream or vegan ice cream.

Simple apple & blackberry crumble

This is a wholesome dessert that's perfect for a cold winter's night.
It's also generous enough to serve at your next dinner party. I love the crunch of the
crumble and it tastes so good paired with a creamy vegan ice cream.

Serves 4–6

4 granny smith apples (about 400 g)
125 g blackberries
2 tablespoons freshly squeezed lemon juice
2 tablespoons coconut sugar
⅓ teaspoon ground cinnamon

Crumble topping
100 g (1 cup) rolled oats
150 g (1 cup) wholemeal flour
2 tablespoons hemp seeds
30 g (½ cup) coconut flakes
60 g (⅓ cup) coconut sugar
125 g (½ cup) vegan butter, chopped

To serve (optional)
natural coconut yoghurt
vegan vanilla ice cream
oat pouring cream

Preheat the oven to 160°C fan-forced. Line a baking tray with paper and lightly grease a 20 cm baking dish.

Place the crumble topping ingredients in a large bowl and use your fingers to rub the vegan butter through the dry ingredients to form a rough crumble. Transfer to the prepared tray and spread out in an even layer. Bake for 7 minutes or until lightly toasted.

Meanwhile, peel, core and julienne the apples and place them in the baking dish with the blackberries, lemon juice, coconut sugar and cinnamon. Toss together to coat all of the fruit in the sugar mixture.

Scatter the crumble topping over the fruit and spread it out in an even layer. Transfer to the oven and bake for 30 minutes or until the crumble is golden and crisp.

Serve the crumble warm by itself or with coconut yoghurt, vegan ice cream or oat cream.

ginger–caramel pudding

I'm just going to say it – I think this ginger–caramel pudding is the perfect Christmas dessert. Naturally sweetened with maple syrup and medjool dates, it is deliciously sweet and has a warm kick from the ginger. It was an absolute hit with my family; I hope you love it as much as we do.

Serves 4

150 g (1 cup) wholemeal flour
1 teaspoon bicarbonate of soda
1 teaspoon baking powder
¼ teaspoon sea salt
250 ml (1 cup) soy milk
1 tablespoon chia seeds
1 teaspoon vanilla extract
2 tablespoons maple syrup
6 medjool dates, pitted
1 tablespoon finely grated ginger
3 tablespoons olive oil
vegan vanilla ice cream or natural coconut
  yoghurt, to serve

Caramel sauce

3 tablespoons maple syrup
2 tablespoons vegan butter
125 ml (½ cup) soy milk
¼ teaspoon sea salt
¼ teaspoon vanilla extract

Preheat the oven to 170°C fan-forced. Line a 15 cm × 10 cm baking tin with baking paper.

Sift the flour, bicarbonate of soda, baking powder and salt into a large bowl. Make a well in the centre and set aside.

Place the soy milk, chia seeds, vanilla extract, maple syrup, dates, ginger and olive oil in a food processor or blender and blend for 45 seconds or until smooth. Pour into the dry ingredients and mix gently until just combined.

Transfer to the prepared tin and bake for 25 minutes.

While the pudding is baking, prepare the caramel sauce by placing all of the ingredients in a small saucepan over medium–high heat. Cook, stirring occasionally, for 15 minutes, until slightly thickened.

Remove the pudding from the oven and allow it to rest for 5 minutes. Pour over half the caramel sauce, then return the tin to the oven and bake for a further 20 minutes or until a skewer inserted into the pudding comes out clean.

Allow the pudding to rest for 5 minutes before serving warm with the remainder of the caramel sauce and a scoop of vegan ice cream or coconut yoghurt.

Baked lemon
cheesecake

Cheesecake is one of my favourite desserts because it combines creaminess, decadence and a touch of fruity zing. This baked cheesecake has a light lemon flavour and is best served with fresh berries on top – yum! You need to cook the cheesecake the day before you intend to serve it.

Serves 10–12

240 g vegan digestive biscuits
125 g (½ cup) vegan butter, plus extra
  for greasing
300 g vegan cream cheese
1 tablespoon finely grated lemon zest
2 tablespoons freshly squeezed lemon juice
1 teaspoon vanilla extract
165 g (¾ cup) caster sugar
1 tablespoon cornflour
125 ml (½ cup) coconut cream
1 tablespoon solid coconut oil
fresh berries, to serve

Preheat the oven to 160°C fan-forced and grease a 20 cm round cake tin with vegan butter.

Place the vegan digestives and vegan butter in a food processor, then process for 1 minute or until a dough forms. Tip the dough into the prepared tin and press it evenly into the base and around the side.

Rinse out the food processor, then add the cream cheese, lemon zest, lemon juice, vanilla extract, caster sugar, cornflour, coconut cream and coconut oil and process until smooth. Pour the mixture into the cake tin, then tap the tin on the bench a few times to remove any air bubbles.

Bake the cheesecake for 55 minutes, until the top is lightly golden and firm to touch. Switch off the oven, but leave the cheesecake inside for a further hour. Transfer the cheesecake to the fridge to set overnight.

The next day, top the cheesecake with fresh berries, then cut into slices and serve.

Any leftover cheesecake will keep in an airtight container in the fridge for up to 5 days.

Rich choc–avo
mousse

Who doesn't love a silky and creamy chocolate mousse? With a base of avocado and vegan dark chocolate, it makes the perfect end to any meal. Serve with your choice of fresh berries to cut through the richness.

Serves 2 / gf

120 g (¾ cup) vegan dark chocolate chips,
   plus extra to serve
2 avocados, roughly chopped
1 tablespoon cacao powder
1 tablespoon maple syrup
1 teaspoon vanilla extract
½ teaspoon sea salt
fresh berries of your choice, to serve

Place the chocolate chips in a microwave-safe bowl and microwave on high for 1½ minutes or until melted.

Place the melted chocolate, avocado, cacao powder, maple syrup, vanilla extract and salt in a blender and blend for 1 minute or until smooth.

Divide the choc–avo mousse between two glasses and place in the fridge for 30 minutes to set.

To serve, top with some fresh berries and extra vegan choc chips.

Nana's baked
rice pudding

There is something so nostalgic about a baked rice pudding. I love making this delicious, creamy dessert – it's so easy to put together and is always a crowd-pleaser! The cinnamon and vanilla add a subtle warmth, which makes this a wonderful after-dinner treat for a cold winter's night.

Serves 4 / gf

200 g (1 cup) medium-grain rice
1 litre (4 cups) soy milk
1 teaspoon vanilla extract
¼ teaspoon ground nutmeg
¼ teaspoon ground cinnamon
¼ teaspoon sea salt
2 tablespoons white sugar
1 teaspoon freshly squeezed lemon juice

To serve (optional)
vegan vanilla ice cream or pouring cream
ground cinnamon

Preheat the oven to 180°C fan-forced.

Place a large flameproof casserole dish or saucepan over medium heat. Add the rice, soy milk, vanilla extract, nutmeg, cinnamon, salt and three-quarters of the sugar. Bring to a simmer, then reduce the heat to low and cook, stirring frequently, for about 10 minutes, until the rice is partially cooked but still slightly crunchy.

Transfer the rice mixture to a small baking dish if you've used a saucepan. Sprinkle the remaining sugar over the top, then transfer the pudding to the oven and bake for 15 minutes or until golden and bubbling on top.

Serve the rice pudding warm with vegan ice cream or pouring cream and a sprinkle of extra ground cinnamon, if desired.

Classic vanilla
birthday cake

There is nothing quite like a classic vanilla birthday cake, is there? This recipe is perfect for your next celebration – or even just a fun weekend treat! While the sprinkles are optional, I think they add a lot of fun to this cake.

Serves 10–12

375 ml (1½ cups) soy milk
2 teaspoons apple cider vinegar
125 ml (½ cup) aquafaba (see Tip)
125 g (½ cup) vegan butter, cubed and
   softened
2 tablespoons olive oil
330 g (1½ cups) caster sugar
1 tablespoon vanilla extract
375 g (2½ cups) plain flour
1 tablespoon baking powder
½ teaspoon sea salt

Preheat the oven to 170°C fan-forced. Grease three 20 cm round cake tins and line them with baking paper.

Combine the soy milk and apple cider vinegar in a bowl and set aside.

Using electric beaters, whisk the aquafaba in a large bowl on medium–high speed for 1 minute or until fluffy. Add the vegan butter, olive oil, caster sugar and vanilla extract and beat for another minute. Sift in the dry ingredients and add the milk mixture, then mix on low speed for about 1 minute, until just combined.

Divide the batter evenly among the prepared tins and bake for 30 minutes or until golden and a skewer inserted into the middle of the cakes comes out clean. Remove from the oven and allow the cakes to cool in the tins for 20 minutes, then turn out onto a wire rack to cool completely.

Tip

Aquafaba is the liquid from canned chickpeas. One 400 g can of chickpeas will yield about 125 ml (½ cup) of aquafaba.

Sweets & Drinks

Recipe continued over the page >

Classic vanilla birthday cake, continued ⌄

Vanilla icing
625 g (5 cups) icing sugar
250 g (1 cup) vegan butter, cubed and
  softened
1 teaspoon vanilla extract
2 tablespoons soy milk
vegan sprinkles, to decorate (optional)

To make the vanilla icing, sift the icing sugar into a large bowl. Add the vegan butter, vanilla extract and soy milk and, using electric beaters, beat for 2–3 minutes, until the icing is light and fluffy.

Place one of the cake layers on a serving plate or cake stand. Ice the top of the cake, then add another cake layer and repeat the process. Place the final layer on top, then ice the side and top of the cake until it is completely covered. Decorate with vegan sprinkles, if desired, then cut into pieces and enjoy.

The cake will keep in an airtight container in the fridge for up to 1 week.

Margaritas,
three ways

Margaritas are my favourite cocktail, especially because they are so versatile and can be made with seemingly endless flavours and garnishes. My three top recipes for a margarita are classic, coconut and spicy – they are all as good as each other, it just depends on your mood. Alternatively, make all three!

Classic

Serves 2

90 ml tequila
75 ml freshly squeezed lime juice
3 cups ice cubes
45 ml Cointreau
1 tablespoon maple syrup
To serve
lime wedge, plus 2 lime slices
coconut sugar
desiccated coconut
sea salt

Coconut

Serves 2

90 ml coconut tequila
75 ml freshly squeezed lime juice
3 cups ice cubes
45 ml Cointreau
1 tablespoon maple syrup
2 tablespoons coconut cream (optional)
To serve
lime wedge
coconut sugar
desiccated coconut
sea salt
toasted coconut flakes

Tip

If you don't have a blender, these cocktails are also great simply shaken and served with chunky ice cubes!

Spicy margarita,
see page 281

Classic margarita

Coconut margarita

Spicy

Serves 2

90 ml tequila
75 ml freshly squeezed lime juice
3 cups ice cubes
45 ml Cointreau
1 tablespoon maple syrup
¼—½ teaspoon Tabasco sauce
To serve
lime wedge
sea salt
dried chilli flakes
2 dried chillies
sriracha chilli sauce

Pick your margarita flavour, add all of the ingredients to a blender and pulse five times.

To serve, run the lime wedge around the rims of two short glasses, then:

For the classic margaritas, dip the rims of the glasses in a little coconut sugar, desiccated coconut and sea salt, then pour in the margarita and top with a slice of lime.

For the coconut margaritas, do the same as above but top with a few toasted coconut flakes instead of lime slices.

For the spicy margaritas, dip the rims of the glasses in a little salt and a few chilli flakes, then pour in the margarita and top with a dried chilli and a touch of sriracha chilli sauce.

CONVERSION CHARTS

Measuring cups and spoons may vary slightly from one country to another, but the difference is generally not enough to affect a recipe. All cup and spoon measures are level.

One Australian metric measuring cup holds 250 ml (8 fl oz), one Australian metric tablespoon holds 20 ml (4 teaspoons) and one Australian metric teaspoon holds 5 ml. North America, New Zealand and the UK use a 15 ml (3-teaspoon) tablespoon.

LENGTH

METRIC	IMPERIAL
3 mm	⅛ inch
6 mm	¼ inch
1 cm	½ inch
2.5 cm	1 inch
5 cm	2 inches
18 cm	7 inches
20 cm	8 inches
23 cm	9 inches
25 cm	10 inches
30 cm	12 inches

LIQUID MEASURES

ONE AMERICAN PINT	ONE IMPERIAL PINT
500 ml (16 fl oz)	600 ml (20 fl oz)

CUP	METRIC	IMPERIAL
⅛ cup	30 ml	1 fl oz
¼ cup	60 ml	2 fl oz
⅓ cup	80 ml	2½ fl oz
½ cup	125 ml	4 fl oz
⅔ cup	160 ml	5 fl oz
¾ cup	180 ml	6 fl oz
1 cup	250 ml	8 fl oz
2 cups	500 ml	16 fl oz
2¼ cups	560 ml	20 fl oz
4 cups	1 litre	32 fl oz

DRY MEASURES

The most accurate way to measure dry ingredients is to weigh them. However, if using a cup, add the ingredient loosely to the cup and level with a knife; don't compact the ingredient unless the recipe requests 'firmly packed'.

METRIC	IMPERIAL
15 g	½ oz
30 g	1 oz
60 g	2 oz
125 g	4 oz (¼ lb)
185 g	6 oz
250 g	8 oz (½ lb)
375 g	12 oz (¾ lb)
500 g	16 oz (1 lb)
1 kg	32 oz (2 lb)

OVEN TEMPERATURES

CELSIUS	FAHRENHEIT
100°C	200°F
120°C	250°F
150°C	300°F
160°C	325°F
180°C	350°F
200°C	400°F
220°C	425°F

CELSIUS	GAS MARK
110°C	¼
130°C	½
140°C	1
150°C	2
170°C	3
180°C	4
190°C	5
200°C	6
220°C	7
230°C	8
240°C	9
250°C	10

THANK YOU!

Creating a cookbook is a huge job and one that I couldn't have done without the help and encouragement of many people. I would like to thank those who have contributed in some form.

To my husband, Alex, thank you for your support during the creation of this book. I wasn't sure I could do it, being a busy mum and running a business, but your encouragement really helped. Thank you also for taking a lot of the parenting load from me during the week and helping me test and taste so many of these recipes.

To my son, Bowie, thank you for inspiring the entire theme for this book, SIMPLE. Life sure is a lot more chaotic with you in it, and simple cooking is a must, but we wouldn't change it for the world. You bring so much joy to our home every single day, and your confusingly honest reviews of the recipes have really kept me on my toes.

To my assistant, Amanda, I really could not have made this book without you. Your organisation and planning skills kept this huge job on track and also kept me motivated during the whole process. You helped to test, try, re-test, cook, shoot and clean up almost every single recipe in this book! Our shoot weeks were crazy and I could not have done it without you.

To my assistant food stylist, Holly, thank you for coming on board for this book to help style and photograph many of the recipes. You are incredibly talented, professional and creative. I am so glad I found your work, and the photos in this book look absolutely incredible thanks to you.

To my Wholesome Store team, Karen, Aimee, Emily and Amy. Thank you for being an important part of our team and really helping to keep The Wholesome Store running smoothly while I focused on this project!

To my wholesome community of followers, thank you for always supporting my recipes and business ventures, for inspiring me to continue to share my life, wholesome recipes and nutrition knowledge. I would not be here living my dream without you guys – thank you so so much!

A special thank you to everyone who supported books number one and two! Publishing these cookbooks is a dream come true, and with your support of *Elsa's Wholesome Life* and *The Global Vegan* I have been able to continue doing what I love, creating delicious plant-based recipes – and a third book! Pinch me, seriously.

The Plum team

To Mary Small, thank you for believing in me in not only making me a published author once, but again and again. I cannot thank you enough for giving me these opportunities, it really is a dream come true and you have been such a pleasure to work with.

To Jane Winning, it has been such a pleasure to work with you again on my third cookbook. Thank you for your support and patience throughout this process and for believing in my vision for it.

To Arielle Gamble, my designer and illustrator, I'm so happy to have you back on my third book. Your beautiful design concepts and illustrations have really tied together all of my cookbooks and made them so beautiful. Thank you also to Heather Menzies for your amazing eye in laying out the book and bringing the imagery together.

To Lucy Heaver, my editor, thank you for being so wonderful with words – you really have improved the flow of my recipes and helped me to build on my skills over the years.

INDEX

Pan Macmillan acknowledges the Traditional Custodians of country throughout Australia and their connections to lands, waters and communities. We pay our respect to Elders past and present and extend that respect to all Aboriginal and Torres Strait Islander peoples today. We honour more than sixty thousand years of storytelling, art and culture.

A PLUM BOOK

First published in 2022 by
Pan Macmillan Australia Pty Limited
Level 25, 1 Market Street,
Sydney, NSW 2000, Australia

Level 3, 112 Wellington Parade,
East Melbourne, VIC 3002, Australia

Design concept and illustrations by Arielle Gamble
Typesetting and layout by Heather Menzies
Editing by Lucy Heaver
Index by Helena Holmgren
Photography by Ellie Bullen (with additional photography by Rob Palmer,
Bec Blooms and Leila Joy)
Prop and food styling by Ellie Bullen and Holly Dyson
Food preparation by Ellie Bullen, Holly Dyson and Amanda Duckworth
Colour reproduction by Splitting Image Colour Studio
Printed and bound in China by Imago Printing International Limited

A CIP catalogue record for this book is available from the National Library of Australia.

We advise that the information contained in this book does not negate personal responsibility on the part of the reader for their own health and safety. It is recommended that individually tailored advice is sought from your healthcare or medical professional. The publishers and their respective employees, agents and authors are not liable for injuries or damage occasioned to any person as a result of reading or following the information contained in this book.

The publisher would like to thank Bilinga Beach Abodes for providing the location for the cover shoot, and Steele and The Wholesome Store for generously providing clothing and props.

10 9 8 7 6 5 4 3 2 1